The Blogger's Edit

Twelve Exclusive
Handknit Designs

MODE
at ROWAN

TIAM SAFARI | KATHARINA VON BLUMENTHAL | SAMANTHA HALL | LILY KATE FRANCE

Welcome

This season we are delighted to welcome bloggers, Kat, Sam, Lily and Tiam to The Blogger's Edit.

As devoted fans from the early days of MODE at Rowan, they have enthusiastically supported our events and knitted our designs.

Taking inspiration from our timeless and easy to wear style, they have chosen their favourite Rowan yarns and designed beautiful garments and accessories that reflect their unique personalities.

This stunning collection of patterns, combining attractive stitch textures with classic shapes are a pleasure to knit and a joy to own.

photographer jesse wild
stylist georgina brant
design layout quail studio
model andreia c
hair & makeup vanessa elles, court-on-camera creatives

First published in Great Britain in 2020 by
Quail Publishing Limited
Old Town Hall, Market Square, Buckingham, Buckinghamshire, MK18 1NJ
E-mail: info@quailstudio.co.uk

ISBN 978-1-9162445-2-8

KATHARINA VON BLUMENTHAL

I started knitting after my eldest daughter was born. Before that, I used to sew a lot but she always wanted to be held and would only sleep on my lap or in my arms, so I used to get very frustrated that I couldn't sew. I needed a hobby that I could do with a baby on my lap.

My first proper knitting project was a jumper from a knitting kit and since then, I knit anywhere and everywhere. Any spare time I have I spend knitting; in the car (if I'm not driving!), in bed, on the sofa, at the playground, and lately even whilst I'm cooking. Have you heard the expression, "if I'm sitting, I'm knitting"? Well, that's me!

I love minimal, clean shapes and for my MODE at Rowan designs I really wanted to showcase the beautiful yarns by keeping things simple. I love the way lace knitting instantly gets a modern vibe when it's combined with really chunky yarn and so the Valentina was born - a simple roll neck with a lovely textured lace panel at the front and moss stitch sleeves, which really enhance the sumptuous softness of Big Wool.

For Lola, a classic raglan jumper, I wanted the real focal point to be the beautiful fabric that is created by combining Alpaca Classic and Kidsilk Haze. To keep things timeless and minimal, nothing beats stockinette stitch and a great fit, ensuring this jumper will be a staple in any wardrobe for many years to come.

LOLA
Page 24 / Anleitung 52

VALENTINA
Page 31 / Anleitung 59

LILY KATE FRANCE

The short story: I picked up the needles at age 8 and haven't put them down since. The long story: I was taught the basics of knitting by my Mum and Nan, fell in love with the stitches very quickly, and after making a few bizarre toys and doll clothes (patchwork tortoise, anyone?), I soon wanted to begin making garments for myself. At age 11, being adult height and child size meant most conventional patterns didn't fit me, so I wrote my own. From then I really was hooked!

I stepped back from designing for a few years during my teens to focus on textiles studies, but now in my early twenties, I've come full circle and knitwear design is a big part of my life again.

My designs for this brochure are in my signature style of 'classic with a twist' - or at least I'd like to think so! Yarn textures often provide the inspiration for me, so I designed items that showcase each yarn to its best. Brioche is such a lovely texture to work with, and the scale of Big Wool meant that simple increases and decreases had a bold impact. I love the feel and palette of Kid Classic, so designed a cardigan with three complimentary colours that can be worn layered or as a statement piece on its own. Brushed Fleece has such a unique, light feel that holds 3D shapes so well, so I made use of this with a rumpled fabric on the collar and cuffs. Nothing says 'cosy winter' like a fluffy hat, and holding two strands of Kidsilk Haze together with one strand of Alpaca Classic was a fun way to make the brim of my Dimple hat extra fuzzy.

 @lilykatemakes

DIMPLE
Page 26 / Anleitung 54

RUMPLED
Page 40 / Anleitung 68

MIDWAY
Page 34 / Anleitung 62

SWERVE SCARF AND BEANIE
Page 44 - 46 / Anleitung 72 - 74

SAMANTHA HALL

I learnt to knit as a child but never got past garter stitch. It was not until about 8 years ago when I picked up knitting needles again that a world of creative possibilities opened up to me. I found it amazing that with the same ball of yarn and a pair of needles, different textures, patterns and shapes could be created. Knitting is magic! I was drawn to designing my own knitwear as I found the creative journey of turning an idea into reality, challenging and so rewarding.

It is a pleasure to have the opportunity to create designs and patterns to help others tap into their own creativity by knitting beautiful items themselves. Seeing a garment come to life within your own hands is wonderful.

My design style is based on classic shapes with subtle details, either with yarn choice or stitch pattern. I create designs that confident beginners can make, and advanced knitters will find appealing. My designs for this collection are based on my desire to create versatile garments that will effortlessly slip into any wardrobe, quickly becoming a much-loved staple.

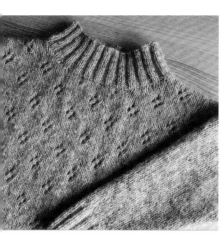 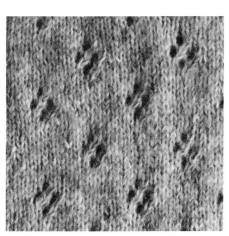 

PEARL
Page 36 / Anleitung 64

HAZEL
Page 30 / Anleitung 58

DARCY
Page 27 / Anleitung 55

TIAM SAFARI

I'm a self-confessed yarn lover, creating knit, crochet and macramé designs with a modern edge. I returned to crafts during a stressful time in my day job, and found that it allowed me to focus on something positive and creative, with the bonus that my projects often resulted in something wearable!

Favouring on-trend pieces that whip up quickly and as seamlessly as possible, my designs vary from chunky cardigans to cotton tops, socks and accessories to Christmas decorations. My pieces for Mode at Rowan use stitch texture on simple shapes to create modern pieces that will be a joy to both knit and wear.

My work has been featured in Vogue Australia and Elle Belgium, and I have produced designs for various yarn brands and magazines.

I live in London with my husband, daughter and two equally string-obsessed cats.

@knitsafari

20

COCOON
Page 42 / Anleitung 70

HERRINGBONE
Page 38 / Anleitung 66

LOLA ●●●

SIZE

To fit bust	81-86	91-97	102-107	112-117	122-127	cm
	32-34	36-38	40-42	44-46	48-50	in
Actual bust measurement of garment						
	90	100	110	120	130	cm
	36	40	44	48	52	in

YARN

Rowan Alpaca Classic (photographed in Dusk 130)

	8	9	9	10	11	× 25g balls

Rowan Kidsilk Haze (photographed in Shadow 653)

	4	5	5	6	6	× 25g balls

NEEDLES

2 × 3.25mm (no 10) (US 3) circular needles 40cm in length
3.25 (no 10) (US 3) double-pointed needles
3.5mm (no 9) (US 4) circular needle 80cm in length
4mm (no 8) (US 6) circular needles 40 and 80cm in length
4mm (no 8) (US 6) double-pointed needles

EXTRAS

Stitch markers
Stitch holders
Waste yarn for Provisional Cast-on

TENSION

20 sts and 24 rounds to 10 cm measured over st st using 4mm (US 6) needles using 1 strand of each yarn.

SPECIAL ABBREVIATIONS

M1R (Make 1 with Right Twist): Insert left-hand needle from back to front under the horizontal loop between the last stitch worked and next stitch on left-needle. Knit into the front loop to twist the stitch—one stitch increased.

M1L (Make 1 with Left Twist): Insert left-hand needle from front to back under the horizontal loop between the last stitch worked and next stitch on left needle. Knit into the back loop to twist the stitch—one stitch increased.

NOTES

- Jumper is worked in one piece, from neck edge down.
- When yoke is complete, body is joined in one piece and worked in rounds (x2). Sleeves are worked in rnds on double-pointed needles.
- One strand of A and one strand of B are held together throughout.

NECKBAND

Using shorter 3.25mm (US 3) circular needle and oddment of waste yarn, cast on 112 [120: 124: 128: 132] sts. Join to work in the round, being careful not to twist. Place marker for beg of round.

Round 1: Knit.
Rep round 1 once more.
Break off waste yarn and join working yarn. Holding a strand of each yarn together, work as folls:
Round 1 (RS): *K1, P1, rep from * around.
This round forms rib.
Cont in rib for 4 cm.
Turning round: Purl.
Next round: *K1, P1, rep from * around.
Cont in rib for 4 cm.
Carefully remove waste yarn and place live sts on spare 3.25mm (US 3) circular needle. Fold neckband in half along turning round to WS and work as folls:
Next (joining round): *Knit next st together with corresponding st from cast-on round, rep from * around.
112 [120: 124: 128: 132] sts.

YOKE

Change to shorter 4mm (US 6) circular needle.
Set-up round: *K1, PM, K36 [40: 42: 44: 46], PM, K1, PM, K18, PM, rep from * once more, omitting last PM of second rep.
Round 1: *K1, SM, M1L, knit to next marker, M1R, SM, K1, SM, M1L, knit to next marker, M1R, SM, rep from * once more, omitting last SM of second rep. [8 sts inc]. 120 [128: 132: 136: 140] sts.

Round 2: Knit.
Rep last 2 rounds 22 [23: 21: 22: 21] times more, changing to longer circular needle when sts no longer fit comfortably on shorter needle. 296 [312: 300: 312: 308] sts.
3rd (4th, 5th) sizes only
Next round: *K1, SM, M1L, knit to next marker, M1R, SM, K1, SM, M1L, knit to next marker, M1R, SM, rep from * once more, omitting last SM of second rep. [8 sts inc]. 308 [320: 316] sts.
Next round: Knit.
Next round: *K1, SM, M1L, knit to next marker, M1R, SM, K1, SM, knit to next marker, SM, rep from * once more, omitting last SM of second rep. [4 sts inc]. 312 [324: 320] sts.
Next round: Knit.
Rep last 4 rounds 1 [2: 4] times more. 324 [348: 368] sts.

All Sizes
Remove markers.

Divide for Sleeves and Body:
Next round: K84 [90: 96: 104: 112] sts for back. Slip next 64 [66: 66: 70: 72] sts onto scrap yarn for left sleeve. Cast on 6 [10: 14: 16: 18] sts for underarm. K84 [90: 96: 104: 112] sts for front. Slip next 64 [66: 66: 70: 72] sts onto scrap yarn for right sleeve. Cast on 6 [10: 14: 16: 18] sts for underarm, placing marker after 3rd [5th: 7th: 8th: 9th] st for beg of round. Join in round. 180 [200: 220: 240: 260] sts for body.

BODY
Knit even in rounds on these 180 [200: 220: 240: 260] sts until body from underarm meas 26 [26: 27: 28: 28] cm.
Change to size 3.5mm (US 4) circular needle.
Next round: *K1, P1, rep from * around.
Cont in rib for 5 cm.
Cast off loosely in rib.

SLEEVES
Slip 64 [66: 66: 70: 72] sts from scrap yarn onto 4mm (US 6) double-pointed needles. Pick up and K6 [10: 14: 16: 18] sts along underarm, placing marker after 3rd [5th: 7th: 8th: 9th] st for beg of round. Divide sts evenly between 4 needles and join in round. 70 [76: 80: 86: 90] sts.
Knit even in rounds until sleeve from underarm meas 34 [34: 35.5: 35.5: 35.5] cm.
Next round: K2tog 17 [19: 20: 21: 22] times, K2 [- : - : 2: 2], K2tog 17 [19: 20: 21: 22] times. 36 [38: 40: 44: 46] sts.
Change to 3.25mm (US 3) double-pointed needles.
Next round: *K1, P1, rep from * around.
Cont in rib for 10 cm.
Turning round: Purl.
Next round: *K1, P1, rep from * around.
Cont in rib for 10 cm.
Cast off loosely in rib.

MAKING UP
Press as described on the information page.
Fold sleeve hem to WS along turning round and slip st loosely in place.

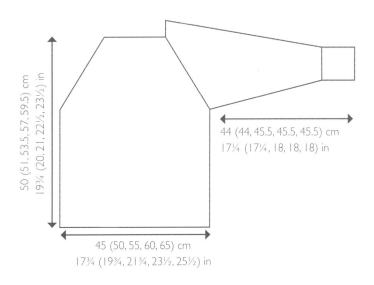

50 (51, 53.5, 57, 59.5) cm
19¾ (20, 21, 22½, 23½) in

44 (44, 45.5, 45.5, 45.5) cm
17¼ (17¼, 18, 18, 18) in

45 (50, 55, 60, 65) cm
17¾ (19¾, 21¾, 23½, 25½) in

DIMPLE •

SIZE
To fit average sized woman's head

YARN
Rowan Alpaca Classic (photographed in Soft Satin 116)
2 x 25gm

Rowan Kidsilk Haze (photographed in White 612)
1 x 25gm

NEEDLES
3.75mm (no 9) (US 5) double pointed needles

TENSION
23 sts and 31 rows to 10cm over st st with Alpaca Classic
using 3.75mm (US 5) needles

SPECIAL ABBREVIATIONS
Make knot (MK): (k1, p1, k1, p1, k1) loosely into next
stitch, then with point of left hand needle pass the 2nd, 3rd,
4th and 5th stitches on right hand needle separately over the
last stitch made, completing knot.

HAT
Using double-pointed 3.75mm needles and holding 1 strand
of Alpaca Classic together with 2 strands of Kidsilk Haze,
cast on 100 sts. Distribute sts evenly over 3 of the 4
needles. Place marker and join to begin working in the
round, taking care not to twist.
Round 1: *K1, P1, rep from * around.
Rep last round 13 times more, inc 4 sts evenly on last
round. 104 sts

Next round: Knit.
Break both strands of KSH and continue with Alpaca
Classic only.
Knit 16 rounds straight.
You will now begin working knot stitch pattern as follows:

Round 1: (MK, K7) to end.
Rounds 2-4: Knit.
Round 5: (K4, MK, K3) to end.
Rounds 6-8: Knit.
Repeat rounds 1-8, 4 times more (5 repeats total, 40
rounds
in pattern).
Next round: (MK, K3, S2tog, K1, psso, K1) to end. 78 sts.
Knit 3 rounds.
Next round: (K2, MK, S2tog, K1, psso) to end. 52 sts.
Knit 3 rounds.
Next round: (MK, S2tog, K1, psso) to end. 26 sts.
Next round: K2tog around. 13 sts.
Next round: K1, K2tog around. 7 sts.
Break yarn and thread onto a tapestry needle, draw yarn
through remaining 7 sts, pull taught and bring yarn end
through to the inside. Weave in all ends and block.

DARCY ••

SIZE

To fit bust	81-86	91-97	102-107	112-117	122-127	cm
	32-34	36-38	40-42	44-46	48-50	in
Actual bust measurement of garment						
	88	98	108	118	128	cm
	34¾	38½	42½	46½	50½	in

YARN

Rowan Alpaca Classic (photographed in Snowflake White 111)

	11	12	12	13	14	x 25gm

Rowan Kidsilk Haze (photographed in White 612)

	6	6	6	7	7	x 25gm

NEEDLES

1 pair size 3.5mm (no 10/9) (US 4) needles
1 pair size 4mm (no 8) (US 6) needles

EXTRAS

Stitch markers
Stitch holders

TENSION

20 sts and 26 rows to 10 cm measured over st st using 4mm (US 6) needles and holding 1 strand of Rowan Kid Classic and 1 strand of Alpaca Classic yarns together.

BACK

Using 3.5mm (US 4) needles and 1 strand of each yarn held together throughout, cast on 126 [140: 154: 168: 182] sts.
Row 1 (RS): K1, *P1, K1, rep from * to last st, K1.
Row 2: K1, *P1, K1, rep from * to last st, K1.
These 2 rows form rib.
Cont in rib until work meas 4 cm, ending with RS facing for next row.
Change to 4mm (US 6) needles.
Next row (RS): K to end, dec 36 [40: 44: 48: 52] sts evenly across. 90 [100: 110: 120: 130] sts.
Starting with a P row, work in st st until work meas 35 [36: 37: 38: 39] cm, ending with RS facing for next row.
Shape armholes
Cast off 3 sts at beg of next 2 rows. 84 [94: 104: 114: 124] sts.
Next row (RS): K1, SSK, K to last 3 sts, K2tog, K1.
Next row: Purl.
Rep the last 2 rows once more. 80 [90: 100: 110: 120] sts.
Cont straight in st st until work meas 21 [22: 23: 24: 25] cm from beg of armhole shaping, ending with RS facing for next row.
Shape right back neck and shoulder
Next row (RS): K24 [28: 32: 36: 40], turn and work on these sts only.

Next row: Cast off 2 sts, P to end.
Next row: Cast off 6 [8: 9: 10: 12] sts, K to end.
Rep last 2 rows once more. 8 [8: 10: 12: 12] sts.
Work 1 row.
Cast off.
Shape left back neck and shoulder
With RS facing, rejoin yarn and cast off centre 32 [34: 36: 38: 40] sts, K to end.
24 [28: 32: 36: 40] sts.
Complete to match first side, reversing shapings.

LEFT FRONT

Using 3.5mm (US 4) needles and 1 strand of each yarn held together throughout, cast on 103 [117: 131: 145: 159] sts.
Next row: *K1, P1, rep from * to last st, K1.
Next row: *P1, K1, rep from * to last st, K1.
These 2 rows forms rib.
Cont in rib until work meas 4 cm, ending with RS facing for next row.
Change to 4mm (US 6) needles.
Next row (RS): Rib to last 7 sts, dec 26 [30: 34: 38: 42] sts evenly across, PM, rib 7. 77 [87: 97: 107: 117] sts.
Work in patt
Next row (WS): Rib 7, SM, P to end.
Next row (RS): K to marker, SM, rib 7.
These 2 rows form st st with rib band patt.
Patt until work is 40 [42: 44: 48: 50] fewer rows than back to armhole shaping, ending with RS facing for next row.

Shape front neck
1st size only
Next row (RS, dec): K to 2 sts before marker, K2tog, SM, rib 7.
Work 3 further rows.
Rep last 4 rows twice more. 74 sts.

2nd, 3rd, 4th & 5th sizes only
Next row (RS, dec): K to 3 sts before marker, K3tog, SM, rib 7.
Work 1 row.
Next row (RS, dec): K to 2 sts before marker, K2tog, SM, rib 7.
Work 1 row.
Rep last 4 rows - [4: 6: 10] more times. 84 [82: 86: 84] sts.

All sizes
Next row (RS, dec): K to 2 sts before marker, K2tog, SM, rib 7.
Work 1 row.
Rep last 2 rows 13 [18: 11: 9: 2] more times. 60 [65: 70: 76: 81] sts.
Shape armhole
Next row (RS): Cast off 3 sts, K to 2 sts before marker, K2tog, SM, rib 7. 56 [61: 66: 72: 77] sts.
Work 1 row.
Next row (RS): K1, ssk, K to 2 sts before marker, K2tog, SM, rib 7.
Work 1 row.
Rep the last 2 rows once more. 52 [57: 62: 68: 73] sts.
Cont in patt, dec 1 st at neck marker as before on next row and on 24 [25: 26: 28: 29] foll alt rows. 27 [31: 35: 39: 43] sts.
Cont, if necessary, until work meas length of back to start of shoulder shaping ending with RS facing for next row.
Shape shoulders
Next row (RS): Cast off 6 [8: 9: 10: 12] sts, K to marker, SM, rib 7.
Next row: Rib 7, SM, P to end.
Rep last 2 rows once more. 15 [15: 17: 19: 19] sts.
Next row: Cast off 8 [8: 10: 12: 12] sts, rm, rib 7. 7 sts.
Next row: Rib 7.
Slip rem 7 sts onto a st holder for neckband.

RIGHT FRONT
Using 3.5mm (US 4) needles and 1 strand of each yarn held together throughout, cast on 103 [117: 131: 145: 159] sts.
Next row: *K1, P1, rep from * to last st, K1.
Next row: K1, *P1, K1, rep from * to end.
These 2 rows forms rib.
Cont in rib until work meas 4 cm, ending with RS facing for next row.
Change to 4mm (US 6) needles.
Next row (RS): Rib 7, PM, K to end, dec 26 [30: 34: 38: 42] sts evenly across. 77 [87: 97: 107: 117] sts.
Work in patt
Next row (WS): P to marker, SM, rib 7.
Next row (RS): Rib 7, SM, K to end.
These 2 rows form st st with rib band patt.
Patt until work is 40 [42: 44: 48: 50] fewer rows than back to armhole shaping, ending with RS facing for next row.
Shape front neck
1st size only
Next row (RS, dec): Rib 7, SM, SSK, K to end.
Work 3 further rows.

Rep last 4 rows twice more. 74 sts.

2nd, 3rd, 4th & 5th sizes only

Next row (RS, dec): Rib 7, SM, SSSK, K to end.

Work 1 row.

Next row (RS, dec): Rib 7, SM, SSK, K to end.

Work 1 row.

Rep last 4 rows - [4: 6: 10] more times. 84 [82: 86: 84] sts.

All sizes

Next row (RS, dec): Rib 7, SM, SSK, K to end.

Work 1 row.

Rep last 2 rows 13 [18: 11: 9: 2] more times. 60 [65: 70: 76: 81] sts.

Shape armholes

Next row (RS, dec): Rib 7, SM, SSK, K to end.

Next row (WS): Cast off 3 sts, P to end. 56 [61: 66: 72: 77] sts.

Next row (RS): Rib 7, SM, SSK, K to last 3 sts, K2tog, K1.

Work 1 row.

Rep the last 2 rows once more. 52 [57: 62: 68: 73] sts.

Cont in patt, dec 1 st at neck marker as before on next row and on 24 [25: 26: 28: 29] foll alt rows. 27 [31: 35: 39: 43] sts.

Cont, if necessary, until work meas length of back to start of shoulder shaping ending with WS facing for next row.

Shape shoulders

Next row (WS): Cast off 6 [8: 9: 10: 12] sts, P to marker, SM, rib 7.

Next row: Rib 7, SM, K to end.

Rep last 2 rows once more. 15 [15: 17: 19: 19] sts.

Next row: Cast off 8 [8: 10: 12: 12] sts, rm, rib 7. 7 sts.

Next row: Rib 7.

Slip rem 7 sts onto a st holder for neckband.

SLEEVES

Using 3.5mm (US 4) needles and 1 strand of each yarn held together throughout, cast on 56 [60: 68: 72: 80] sts.

Row 1 (RS): K1, *P1, K1, rep from * to last st, K1.

Row 2: K1, *P1, K1, rep from * to last st, K1.

These 2 rows form rib.

Cont in rib until work meas 9 cm, ending with RS facing for next row.

Change to 4mm (US 6) needles.

Next row (RS): Knit to end, inc 10 [10: 8: 8: 6] sts evenly across. 66 [70: 76: 80: 86] sts.

Cont in st st, inc 1 st at each end of 9th [9th: 8th: 8th: 7th] and every foll 10th [10th: 12th: 12th: 14th] rows to 84 [88: 92: 96: 100] sts.

Cont straight in st st until sleeve meas 50 [51: 52: 53: 54] cm, ending with RS facing for next row.

Shape sleeve top

Cast off 3 sts at beg of next 2 rows. 78 [82: 86: 90: 94] sts.

Next row (RS): K1, SSK, K to last 3 sts, K2tog, K1.

Next row: Purl.

Rep the last 2 rows once more. 74 [78: 82: 86: 90] sts.

Work 4 rows in st st.

Cast off.

MAKING UP

Press as described on the information page.

Join shoulder seams.

Neckband

With RS facing and using 3.5mm (US 4) needles, cont in patt across 7 sts from left front holder as follows:

Cont in rib as set until band fits halfway around back neck.

Cast off in rib.

Rep for 7 sts from right front holder.

Join band seam and sew band in place around back neck.

Ties

With RS facing, 3.5mm (US 4) needles and 1 strand of each yarn held together throughout, starting 2.5cm from beg of front neck shaping, pick up and knit 8 sts up right front edge.

Rib row: [K1, P1] 4 times.

This row forms rib.

Rib until tie meas 96.5 [104: 111.5: 119: 126.5] cm or your preferred length.

Cast off in rib.

Rep for left tie starting at front neck shaping down left front edge.

Sew in sleeves.

Join side and sleeve seams, leaving a 3.5 cm gap in right side seam to accommodate left tie.

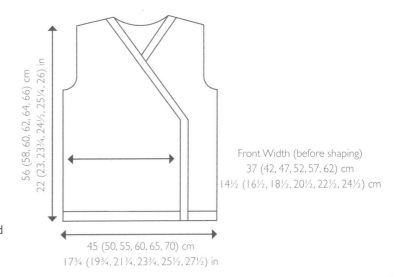

Front Width (before shaping)
37 (42, 47, 52, 57, 62) cm
14½ (16½, 18½, 20½, 22½, 24½) cm

56 (58, 60, 62, 64, 66) cm
22 (23, 23¾, 24½, 25¼, 26) in

45 (50, 55, 60, 65, 70) cm
17¾ (19¾, 21¾, 23¾, 25½, 27½) in

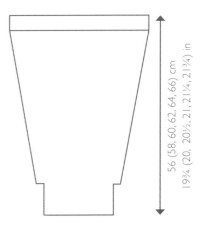

56 (58, 60, 62, 64, 66) cm
19¾ (20, 20½, 21, 21¼, 21¾) in

HAZEL ••

SIZE
46cm wide and 200cm long

YARN
Rowan Big Wool (photographed in Linen 048)
7 x 100gm

NEEDLES
10mm (no 000) (US 15) needles

TENSION
10sts and 12rows to 10 cm over moss stitch pattern using
10mm (US 15) needles

SCARF
Using 10mm (US 15) needles, cast on 46 sts.
Row 1 (RS): K1, P1 to end.
Row 2: K1, P1 to end.
Row 3: P1, K1 to end.
Row 4: P1, K1 to end.
Rows 1 – 4 set pattern.

Work in pattern until scarf measures 200cm, ending on row
2 of pattern.
Cast off.

FINISHING
Press as described on the information page.

VALENTINA ●●●

SIZE

To fit bust	81-86	91-97	102-107	112-117	122-127	cm
	32-34	36-38	40-42	44-46	48-50	in
Actual bust measurement of garment						
	90	100	110	120	130	cm
	35½	39½	43½	47¼	51¼	in

YARN

Rowan Big Wool (photographed in White Hot 001)

	8	9	10	11	12	× 100gm

NEEDLES

8mm (no 0) (US 11) circular needles 80cm in length
8mm (no 0) (US 11) double pointed needles
10mm (no 000) (US 15) circular needles 80cm in length
10mm (no 000) (US 15) double pointed needles

EXTRAS

Stitch markers
Stitch holders

TENSION

10 sts and 16 rows to 10 cm measured over st st using 10mm (US 15) needles.
12 sts and 16 rows to 10 cm measured over moss stitch using 10mm (US 15) needles.

STITCH PATTERNS
Moss stitch (in the round)
Round 1: K1, *P1, K1, rep from * to end.
Round 2: P1, *K1, P1, rep from * to end.
Rep these 2 rounds for patt.

Moss stitch (flat)
Row 1: K1, *P1, K1, rep from * to end.
Rep this row for patt.

Eyelet Fan panel (in the round)
Round 1: K19.
Round 2: Yo, K3tog, K13, K3tog, yo. 17 sts.
Round 3: K17.
Round 4: Yo, K3tog, K11, K3tog, yo. 15 sts.
Round 5: K15.
Round 6: Yo, K3tog, K9, K3tog, yo. 13 sts.
Round 7: K13.
Round 8: Yo, K3tog, [yo, K1] 7 times, yo, K3tog, yo. 19 sts.
Rep Rounds 1-8 for patt.

Eyelet Fan panel (flat)
Row 1 (WS): P19.
Row 2: Yo, K3tog, K13, K3tog, yo. 17 sts.
Row 3: P17.
Row 4: Yo, K3tog, K11, K3tog, yo. 15 sts.
Row 5: P15.
Row 6: Yo, K3tog, K9, K3tog, yo. 13 sts.
Row 7: P13.
Row 8: Yo, K3tog, [yo, K1] 7 times, yo, K3tog, yo. 19 sts.
Rep Rows 1-8 for patt.

PATTERN NOTE
Due to the Eyelet Fan panel, the stitch count changes throughout.

BODY
Using 8mm (US 11) circular needles, cast on 162 (180: 198: 216: 234) sts. Join to work in the round, being careful not to twist. Place marker for beg of round.
Rib round: *K1, P1, rep from * to end.
This round forms rib.
Cont in rib until work meas 5 cm.
Change to 10mm (US 15) needles.
Next round: Knit, dec 72 [78: 88: 94: 104] sts evenly around. 90 [102: 110: 122: 130] sts.

Now work in patt as follows:

Set up round: K12 [15: 17: 20: 22] sts, pm, K1, (P1, K1) twice, PM, [yo, K1] 9 times, yo, PM, K1, (P1, K1) twice, pm, K to end. 100 [112: 120: 132: 140] sts.

Next round: K to marker, SM, P1, (K1, P1) twice, SM, work Round 1 of Eyelet Fan panel, SM, P1, (K1, P1) twice, SM, K to end.

These rounds set patt of st st with Eyelet Fan Panel patt framed with Moss st.

Patt straight until work meas 34 [35: 36: 37: 38] cm, ending after an even-numbered round of Eyelet Fan panel.

Divide for armholes

Row 1 (RS): K to marker, SM, work in moss st to marker, SM, work next row of Eyelet Fan panel, SM, work in moss st to marker, SM, K12 [15: 17: 20: 22] sts, turn and work on these sts only for front, leaving remaining 45 [51: 55: 61: 65] sts on stitch holder.

FRONT

Making sure to adjust Moss st and Eyelet Fan panel to working flat instead of in the round, cont in patt as set until front meas approximately 14 [14: 15: 15: 16] cm from divide, ending after a Row 1 of Eyelet Fan panel. 53 [59: 63: 69: 73] sts.

Shape left front neck and shoulder

Next row (RS): Patt 17 [20: 22: 25: 27], turn and work on these sts only.

Dec 1 st at neck edge on next 3 [4: 4: 4: 4] rows. 14 [16: 18: 21: 23] sts.

Work 3 [2: 2: 2: 2] rows straight.

Cast off.

Shape right front neck and shoulder

With RS facing, slip centre 19 sts onto a st holder, rejoin yarn to rem sts and patt to end. 17 [20: 22: 25: 27] sts.

Complete to match first side, reversing shapings.

BACK

Rejoin yarn to rem 45 [51: 55: 61: 65] sts and cont in st st until back meas same as front before shaping neck, ending with RS facing for next row.

Work 2 further rows in st st.

Shape right back neck and shoulder

Next row (RS): K16 [19: 21: 24: 26] sts, turn and work on these sts only.

Dec 1 st at neck edge on next 2 [3: 3: 3: 3] rows. 14 [16: 18: 21: 23] sts.

Work 2 [1: 1: 1: 1] rows straight.

Cast off.

Shape left back neck and shoulder

With RS facing, rejoin yarn to rem sts and cast off centre 13 sts, K to end. 16 [19: 21: 24: 26] sts.

Complete to match first side, reversing shapings.

SLEEVES

Join shoulder seams using mattress stitch.

Using 10mm (US 15) double pointed needles, starting at centre underarm, pick up and knit 20 [21: 21: 21: 22] sts evenly up to shoulder seam, and pick up and knit 20 [21: 21: 21: 22] sts evenly down from shoulder seam back to centre of underarm. Join to work in the round and place marker for beg of round. 40 [42: 42: 42: 44] sts.

Work in patt as follows:

Round 1: *P1, K1, rep from * to end.
Round 2: *K1, P1, rep from * to end.

These 2 rounds form moss st.

Cont straight in Moss st until sleeve meas 34 [35: 35: 36.5: 36.5] cm.

Next round: *K2tog, rep from * to end. 20 [21: 21: 21: 22] sts.

Change to 8mm (US 11) double pointed needles.

Rib round: *K1, P1, rep from * to end.

This round forms rib.

Work in rib until cuff meas 5 cm.

Cast off loosely in rib.

MAKING UP

Press as described on the information page.

Join shoulder seams using mattress stitch.

Roll neck

With RS facing and using 8mm (US 11) double pointed needles, pick up and knit 9 sts down left front neck, K19 sts from front neck holder, pick up and knit 9 sts up right front neck, pick up and knit 4 sts down right back neck, pick up and knit 13 sts along back neck, pick up and knit 4 sts up left back neck. Join to work in the round and place marker for beg of round. 58 sts.

Rib round: *K1, P1, rep from * to end.

This round forms rib.

Cont in rib until neck meas 10 cm.

Change to 10mm (US 15) double pointed needles.

Cont in rib until neck meas 20 cm.

Cast off loosely in rib.

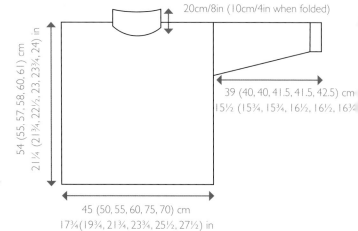

20cm/8in (10cm/4in when folded)

54 (55, 57, 58, 60, 61) cm
21¼ (21¾, 22½, 23, 23¾, 24) in

39 (40, 40, 41.5, 41.5, 42.5) cm
15½ (15¾, 15¾, 16½, 16½, 16¾

45 (50, 55, 60, 75, 70) cm
17¾ (19¾, 21¾, 23¾, 25½, 27½) in

MIDWAY ●●

SIZE

To fit bust	81-86	91-97	102-107	112-117	122-127	cm
	32-34	36-38	40-42	44-46	48-50	in
Actual bust measurement of garment						
	101.5	111.5	121.5	134	143.5	cm
	40	44	48	52¾	56½	in

YARN

Rowan Kid Classic

A Pumice 888						
	4	4	5	5	5	x 50gm
B Feather 828						
	1	1	1	1	1	x 50gm
C Cement 890						
	1	1	1	2	2	x 50gm

NEEDLES

1 pair 4mm (no 8) (US 6) needles
4mm (no 8) (US 6) double pointed needles
1 pair 5.5mm (no 5) (US 9) needles
5.5mm (no 5) (US 9) double pointed needles

EXTRAS

Waste yarn or spare needles
1 stitch holder
5 buttons

TENSION

16 sts and 24 rows to 10 cm measured over st st using 5.5mm (US 9) needles.

BODY

Using 4mm (US 6) needles and yarn A, cast on 230 [254: 278: 310: 334] sts.
Row 1 (RS): K1, *P2, K2, rep from * to last st, K1.
Row 2: K1, *P2, K2, rep from * to last st, K1.
These 2 rows form rib.
Cont in rib until work meas 5 cm, ending with RS facing for next row.
Change to 5.5mm (US 9) needles.
Next row (RS): K to end, dec 75 [83: 91: 103: 112] sts evenly across. 155 [171: 187: 207: 222] sts.
Starting with a P row, work in st st until work meas 26 [27: 28: 29: 30] cm, ending with RS facing for next row.
Divide for armholes
Next row (RS): K37 [41: 45: 50: 54] sts, place these sts on waste yarn or spare needle for right front, K81 [89: 97: 107: 114] sts, turn and work on these sts only for back, leaving rem 37 [41: 45: 50: 54] sts, sts on waste yarn or spare needle for left front.

BACK

Cont in st st until back meas 18 [18: 19: 19: 20] cm from divide, ending with RS facing for next row.

Shape right back neck and shoulder
Row 1 (RS): K27 [31: 35: 40: 43] sts, turn and work on these sts only.
Row 2: Cast off 3 sts, P to end.
Row 3: Cast off 6 [7: 8: 10: 11] sts, K to end.
Rows 4-5: Rep Rows 2-3. 9 [11: 13: 14: 15] sts.
Row 6: Cast off 3 [3: 3: 3: 4] sts, P to end. 6 [8: 10: 11: 11] sts.
Cast off.
Shape left back neck and shoulder
With RS facing, rejoin yarn to rem sts and cast off centre 27 [27: 27: 27: 28] sts, K to end. 27 [31: 35: 40: 43] sts
Complete to match first side, reversing shapings.

LEFT FRONT

With RS facing, rejoin yarn A to held 37 [41: 45: 50: 54] sts.
Cont in st st until front meas 9 [9: 10: 10: 11] cm from divide, ending with WS facing for next row.
Shape front neck
Next row (WS): Cast off 6 [6: 6: 6: 7] sts at neck edge, P to end.
Work 1 row.
Next row: Cast off 5 [5: 5: 5: 6] sts at neck edge, P to end.
Work 1 row.
Next row: Cast off 4 sts at neck edge, P to end.

Dec 1 st at neck edge on next 3 rows, then on 1 foll alt row. 18 [22: 26: 31: 33] sts.
Work straight in st st until Front measures same as back to shoulder shaping, ending at armhole edge.

Shape shoulders
Cast off 6 [7: 8: 10: 11] sts at beg of next and 1 foll alt row. 6 [8: 10: 11: 11] sts.
Work 1 row.
Cast off.

RIGHT FRONT
With **WS** facing, rejoin yarn A to held 37 [41: 45: 50: 54] sts.
Cont in st st until front meas 9 [9: 10: 10: 11] cm from divide, ending with RS facing for next row.
Complete as for left front, reversing shapings.

SLEEVES
Press as described on the information page.
Join shoulder seams.
Using 5.5mm (US 9) needles and yarn A, starting at centre underarm, pick up and knit 32 [32: 32: 36: 36] sts evenly up to shoulder seam, and pick up and knit 32 [32: 32: 36: 36] sts evenly down from shoulder seam back to centre of underarm. Join to work in the round and place marker to mark beg of round. 64 [64: 64: 72: 72] sts.
Cont in st st for 10 cm.
Change to yarn B.
Work in st st for a further 3 cm.
Change to yarn C.
Cont in st st until sleeve meas 27.5 [28: 28.5: 29: 29] cm.

Shape sleeve
Next round: *K6 [6: 6: 7: 7], K2tog, rep from * to end.
56 [56: 56: 64: 64] sts.
Next round: Knit.
Next round: *K5 [5: 5: 6: 6], K2tog, rep from * to end.
48 [48: 48: 56: 56] sts.
Next round: Knit.
Next round: K to end, dec 4 [0: 0: 4: 4] sts evenly around.
44 [48: 48: 52: 52] sts.

Cuff
Change to 4mm (US 6) needles.
Next round: *K2, P2, rep from * to end.
This round forms rib.
Rib until cuff meas 8cm.
Cast off loosely in rib.

MAKING UP
Button band
With RS facing and using 5.5mm (US 9) needles and yarn A, pick up and knit 82 [86: 90: 94: 98] sts down left front.
Row 1 (WS): P2, *K2, P2, rep from * to end.
Row 2: K2, *P2, K2, rep from * to end.
These 2 rows form rib.
Cont in rib until band meas 5cm, ending with RS facing for next row.
Cast off in rib.
Mark front edge to indicate position of 4 buttons, with the first one 2.5cm from cast on edge of body and other 3 evenly spaced along band (noting that 1 further button will be placed 2.5cm up on the neckband).

Buttonhole band
With RS facing and using 5.5mm (US 9) needles and yarn A, pick up and knit 82 [86: 90: 94: 98] sts up right front.
Row 1 (WS): P2, *K2, P2, rep from * to end.
Row 2: K2, *P2, K2, rep from * to end.
These 2 rows form rib.
Cont in rib until band meas 2.5cm, ending with a RS facing for next row.
Buttonhole row (RS): [Work in rib to marked button position, rib2tog, yf] 4 times, rib to end.
Cont in rib as set until band meas 5cm, ending with RS facing for next row.
Cast off in rib.

Neckband
With RS facing and using 5.5mm (US 9) needles and yarn A, pick up and knit 12 sts along row ends of buttonhole band, 37 [37: 37: 37: 41] sts up right front neck, 14 [14: 14: 14: 15] sts down right back neck, 40 [40: 40: 40: 42] sts along back neck, pick up and knit 14 [14: 14: 14: 15] sts up left back neck, 37 [37: 37: 37: 41] sts down left front neck and 12 sts along row ends of button band. 166 [166: 166: 166: 178] sts.
Row 1 (WS): P2, *K2, P2, rep from * to end.
Row 2: K2, *P2, K2, rep from * to end.
These 2 rows form rib.
Cont in rib until band meas 2.5cm, ending with RS facing for next row.
Buttonhole row (RS): Work 6 sts in rib, rib2tog, yf, rib to end.
Cont in rib until band meas 5cm, ending with RS facing for next row.
Cast off in rib.
Sew on buttons.

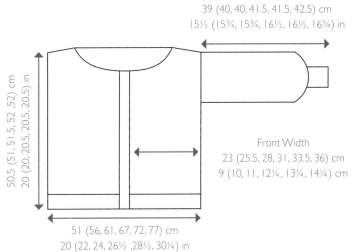

39 (40, 40, 41.5, 41.5, 42.5) cm
15½ (15¾, 15¾, 16½, 16½, 16¾) in

50.5 (51, 51.5, 52, 52) cm
20 (20, 20.5, 20.5, 20.5) in

Front Width
23 (25.5, 28, 31, 33.5, 36) cm
9 (10, 11, 12¼, 13¼, 14¼) cm

51 (56, 61, 67, 72, 77) cm
20 (22, 24, 26½, 28½, 30¼) in

PEARL ••

SIZE

To fit bust	81-86	91-97	102-107	112-117	122-127	cm
	32-34	36-38	40-42	44-46	48-50	in
Actual bust measurement of garment						
	101	116	121	131	146	cm
	40	45½	47½	51½	57½	in

YARN

Rowan Alpaca Classic (photographed in Feather Grey Melange 101)

	13	14	14	15	16	x 25gm

NEEDLES

1 pair size 4mm (no 8) (US 6) needles
1 pair size 5mm (no 6) (US 8) needles

EXTRAS

2 stitch holders
4 stitch markers

TENSION

16 sts and 22 rows to 10 cm measured over pattern/st st using 5mm (US 8) needles and holding 2 strands of Rowan Alpaca Classic held together.

PATTERN NOTE

When working the front shaping for neck and shoulders, if you cannot complete a full 12-st repeat of pattern, work these sts in st st.

BACK

Using 4mm (US 6) needles and 2 strands of Rowan Alpaca Classic yarn held together throughout, cast on 108 [120: 132: 144: 156] sts.
Row 1 (RS): Sl 1, *P2, K2, rep from * to last 3 sts, P2, K1.
Row 2: Sl 1, K2, *P2, K2, rep from * to last st, K1.
These 2 rows form rib.
Cont in rib until work meas 10 cm, ending with RS facing for next row.
Change to 5mm (US 8) needles.
Next row (RS): Knit, dec 27 [27: 35: 39: 39] sts evenly across. 81 [93: 97: 105: 117] sts.
Next row: Purl. **
Cont in st st, starting with a K row, until back meas 32 [33: 34: 35: 36] cm, ending with RS facing for next row.
Place markers at both ends of last row (to denote top of side seam).
Cont in st st until back meas 20 [21: 22: 23: 24] cm from markers, ending with RS facing for next row.
Shape right back neck and shoulder
Row 1 (RS): K27 [33: 34: 38: 43] sts, turn and work on these sts only. 27 [33: 34: 38: 43] sts.

Row 2: Cast off 4 [5: 5: 5: 5] sts, P to end. 23 [28: 29: 33: 38] sts.
Row 3: Cast off 8 [10: 10: 11: 13] sts, K to end. 15 [18: 19: 22: 25] sts.
Row 4: Purl.
Row 5: Cast off 8 [10: 10: 11: 13] sts, K to end. 7 [8: 9: 11: 12] sts.
Row 6: Purl.
Cast off.
Shape left back neck and shoulder
With RS facing, rejoin yarn to rem sts and cast off centre 27 [27: 29: 29: 31] sts, K to end. 27 [33: 34: 38: 43] sts.
Complete to match first side, reversing shapings.

FRONT

Work as for Back to **.
Now work in patt as follows:
Row 1 (RS): K1 [1: 3: 1: 1], *K2, K2tog, yo, K8, rep from * to last 8 [8: 10: 8: 8] sts, K2, K2tog, yo, K4 [4: 6: 4: 4].
Row 2 and foll WS rows: Purl.
Row 3: K1 [1: 3: 1: 1], *K1, [K2tog, yo] twice, K7, rep from * to last 8 [8: 10: 8: 8] sts, K1, (K2tog, yo) twice, K3 [3: 5: 3: 3].
Row 5: As Row 1.
Row 7: Knit.
Row 9: K1 [1: 3: 1: 1], *K8, K2tog, yo, K2, rep from * to last 8 [8: 10: 8: 8] sts, K to end.
Row 11: K1 [1: 3: 1: 1], *K7, [K2tog, yo] twice, K1, rep from * to last 8 [8: 10: 8: 8] sts, K to end.
Row 13: As Row 9.
Row 15: Knit.
Row 16 (WS): Purl.
These 16 rows set patt.

Cont in patt straight until front meas 32 [33: 34: 35: 36] cm, ending with RS facing for next row.
Place markers at both ends of last row (to denote top of side seam).
Cont in main patt until front meas 14 [15: 16: 17: 18] cm from markers, ending with RS facing for next row. When working shaping, if you cannot complete a 12-st repeat of pattern, work these sts in st st.

Shape left side neck
Next row (RS): Patt 32 [37: 39: 43: 48], turn and work on these sts only.
Cont in patt, dec 1 st at neck edge on next and 5 [5: 7: 7: 7] foll rows, then on 3 [3: 2: 2: 2] foll alt rows. 23 [28: 29: 33: 38] sts.
Cont in patt straight until front meas same as back to shoulder shaping, ending with RS facing for next row.
Shape shoulder
Cast off 8 [10: 10: 11: 13] sts at beg of next and foll alt row. 7 [8: 9: 11: 12] sts.
Work 1 row.
Cast off.
Shape right side neck
With RS facing, rejoin yarn to rem sts, cast off centre 17 [19: 19: 19: 21] sts, patt to end. 32 [37: 39: 43: 48] sts.
Complete to match first side, reversing shapings.

SLEEVES
Using 4mm (US 6) needles and 2 strands of Rowan Alpaca Classic yarn held together throughout, cast on 46 [50: 50: 54: 54] sts.
Rib row: K1, *P2, K2, rep from * to last st, K1.
This row forms rib.
Cont in rib until work meas 8 cm, ending with RS facing for next row.
Change to 5mm (US 8) needles.
Next row (RS): Knit, dec 10 [10: 10: 12: 12] sts evenly across. 36 [40: 40: 42: 42] sts.
Cont in st st, starting with a P row, for 9 rows, ending with RS facing for next row.
Inc 1 st at each end of next row and every following 4th row until there are 64 [68: 70: 74: 76] sts.
Cont straight in st st until work meas 43 [44: 45: 46: 47] cm, ending with RS facing for next row.
Cast off.

MAKING UP
Press as described on the information page.
Join right shoulder seam using mattress stitch.
Collar
With RS facing and using 4mm (US 6) needles and 2 strands of Rowan Alpaca Classic yarn held together throughout, starting at top left front neck and ending at top left back neck, pick up and knit 118 [126: 130: 134: 146] sts evenly around neck opening. 118 [126: 130: 134: 146] sts.
Rib row: K1, *K2, P2, rep from * to last st, K1.
This row forms rib.
Cont straight in rib until work meas 8 cm, ending with RS facing for next row.
Cast off loosely.
Join left shoulder and collar seam.
Sew cast off edge of sleeve between markers on back and front.
Join side seams between marker and top of hem only. Join sleeve seams.

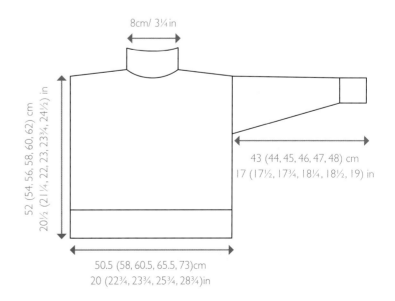

8cm/ 3¼ in

52 (54, 56, 58, 60, 62) cm
20½ (21¼, 22, 23, 23¾, 24½) in

43 (44, 45, 46, 47, 48) cm
17 (17½, 17¾, 18¼, 18½, 19) in

50.5 (58, 60.5, 65.5, 73)cm
20 (22¾, 23¾, 25¾, 28¾)in

HERRINGBONE ●●●

SIZE

To fit bust	81-86	91-97	102-107	112-117	122-127	cm
	32-34	36-38	40-42	44-46	48-50	in
Actual bust measurement of garment						
	90	103	113	123	133	cm
	35½	40½	44½	48½	52½	in

YARN

Rowan Kid Classic (photographed in Floss 899)

	8	8	9	9	10	× 50gm

NEEDLES

1 pair 5.5mm (no 5) (US 9) needles
5.5mm(no 5) (US 9) circular needle 80cm in length

EXTRAS

Stitch holders
3 stitch markers

TENSION

18 sts and 23 rows to 10 cm measured over st st using 5.5mm (US 9) needles.
28 sts and 24 rows to 10 cm measured over Herringbone st patt using 5.5mm (US 9) needles.

STITCH PATTERN
Herringbone st
Row 1 (RS): Sl1, *K tbl in second st on LH needle without dropping st off needle, then K tbl in first st and allow both sts to drop from LH needle, rep from * to end.
Row 2 (WS): Sl1, *P second st on LH needle without dropping st off needle, then P first and allow both to drop from LH needle, rep from * to end.
These 2 rows form patt.

BACK
Using 5.5mm (US 9) needles, cast on 109 [123: 135: 147: 159] sts.
Row 1 (RS): Sl 1, * P1, K1 tbl, rep from * to last 2 sts, P1, K1.
Row 2 (WS): Sl 1, K1, *P1 tbl, K1, rep from * to last st, K1.
These 2 rows form rib.
Cont in rib until work meas 7 cm, ending with WS facing for next row.
Next row (WS): Purl, inc 18 [22: 24: 26: 28] sts evenly across. 127 [145: 159: 173: 187] sts. **
Work in Herringbone st patt until back meas 37 [38: 38: 39: 39] cm, ending with a RS facing for next row.
Place markers at both ends of last row (to denote underarm).
Cont in patt a further 48 [48: 50: 50: 52] rows, ending with RS facing for next row.

Shape right back neck and shoulder
Row 1 (RS): Patt 45 [53: 59: 66: 72] sts, turn and work on these sts only.
Row 2: Cast off 3 [3: 3: 4: 4] sts, patt to end. 42 [50: 56: 62: 68] sts.
Row 3: Cast off 8 [10: 12: 13: 15] sts, patt to end. 34 [40: 44: 49: 53] sts.
Row 4: Cast off 3 sts, patt to end. 31 [37: 41: 46: 50] sts.
Row 5: Cast off 8 [10: 12: 13: 15] sts, patt to end. 23 [27: 29: 33: 35] sts.
Row 6: Cast off 2 sts, patt to end. 21 [25: 27: 31: 33] sts.
Row 7: Cast off 9 [11: 12: 14: 15] sts, patt to end. 12 [14: 15: 17: 18] sts.
Row 8: Cast off 2 sts, patt to end. 10 [12: 13: 15: 16] sts.
Cast off.
Shape left back neck and shoulder
With RS facing, rejoin yarn and cast off 37 [39: 41: 41: 43] sts, patt to end. 45 [53: 59: 66: 72] sts.
Complete to match first side, reversing shapings.

FRONT
Work as for back to **.
Work in Herringbone st patt until front meas 15 [16: 17: 18: 19: 20] cm, ending with a RS facing for next row.
Shape left side neck
Next row (RS): Patt 63 [72: 79: 86: 93], turn and work on these sts only.
Cont in patt, dec 1 st at neck edge on next and foll - [- : - : 2: -] rows, then on foll 4th [3rd: 3rd: 3rd: alt] row 3 [4: 4: 3: 5] times. 59 [67: 74: 80: 87] sts.

Patt 2 [2: - : 1: -] further rows ending with RS facing for next row. (16 [16:14: 14: 12] rows worked for neck shaping). Place markers at side edge of last row (to denote underarm).

Work 48 [48: 50: 50: 52] rows, dec 1 st at neck edge on next and every foll alt row 23 [23: 24: 24: 25] times, ending with RS facing for next row. 35 [43: 49: 55: 61] sts.

Front should match length of back to shoulder shaping, ending with RS facing for next row (with **WS** facing for next row for right side neck).

Shape shoulder

Rows 1-2: Patt to end.

Row 3: Cast off 8 [10: 12: 13: 15] sts, patt to end. 27 [33: 37: 42: 46] sts.

Row 4: Patt to end.

Rows 5-6: Rep Rows 3-4. 19 [23: 25: 29: 31] sts.

Row 7: Cast off 9 [11: 12: 14: 15] sts, patt to end. 10 [12: 13: 15: 16] sts.

Row 8: Patt to end.

Cast off.

Shape right side neck

With RS facing, place center st on holder, rejoin yarn to rem sts, patt to end. 63 [72: 79: 86: 93] sts.

Complete to match first side, reversing shapings.

SLEEVES

Using 5.5mm (US 9) needles cast on 48 [52: 58: 62: 68] sts.

Row 1 (RS): K1, *P1, K1 tbl, rep from * to last st, K1.

Row 2 (WS): K1, *P1 tbl, K1, rep from * to last st, K1.

These 2 rows form rib.

Cont in rib until work meas 12 cm, ending with RS facing for next row.

Next row (RS): Knit, dec 12 [12: 14: 16: 18] sts evenly across. 36 [40: 44: 46: 50] sts.

Starting with a P row, work 13 rows in st st, ending with RS facing for next row.

Inc 1 st at each end of next row and every foll alt row 12 [6: 5: 2: 1] times, then every foll 4th [4th: 4th: 4th: 4th] row to 82 [82: 86: 86: 90] sts.

Cont straight in st st until work meas 51 [52: 53: 54: 55] cm, ending with RS facing for next row.

Cast off.

MAKING UP

Press as described on the information page.

Join shoulder seams.

Neckband

With RS facing and using 5.5mm (US 9) circular needle, starting at left shoulder, pick up and knit 55 [55: 55: 57: 57] sts down left neck to centre front, pm, K1 from front neck st holder, pick up and knit 55 [55: 55: 57: 57] sts up right neck, pick up and knit 37 [39: 41: 41: 43] sts across back neck. PM and join to work in the round. 148 [150: 152: 156: 158] sts.

Round 1: P1, (K1 tbl, P1) to marker, SM, K1 tbl, (P1, K1 tbl) to end.

This round sets rib.

Round 2: Work in rib to 1 st before marker, PM, remove old marker, rib to end.

Round 3: Work in rib to 2 sts before marker, K1 tbl, PM, remove old marker, rib to end.

Rounds 4-5: As Rounds 2-3.

Round 6: As Round 2.

Cast off loosely in rib, dec as before at centre front.

Sew cast off edge of sleeve between markers on back and front. Join side and sleeve seams, reversing sleeve cuff seam halfway for turnback.

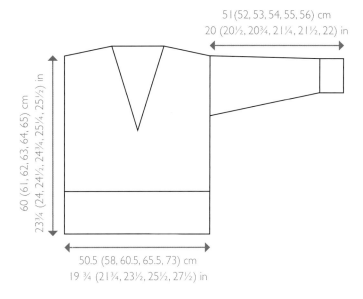

51 (52, 53, 54, 55, 56) cm
20 (20½, 20¾, 21¼, 21½, 22) in

60 (61, 62, 63, 64, 65) cm
23¾ (24, 24½, 24¾, 25¼, 25½) in

50.5 (58, 60.5, 65.5, 73) cm
19 ¾ (21¾, 23½, 25½, 27½) in

RUMPLED ••

Lily

SIZE

To fit bust	81-86	91-97	102-107	112-117	122-127	cm
	32-34	36-38	40-42	44-46	48- 50	in
Actual bust measurement of garment						
	100	110	120	130	140	cm
	40	44	48	52	56	in

YARN

Rowan Brushed Fleece (photographed in Cove 251)

	7	8	9	10	11	x 50gm

NEEDLES

5mm (no 6) (US 8) circular needles 40cm and 80cm in length
5mm (no 6) (US 8) double pointed needles
6mm (no 3) (US 10) circular needle 40cm in length
7mm (no 2) (US 10.5/11) circular needle 80cm in length
7mm (no 2) (US 10.5/11) double-pointed needles

EXTRAS

Stitch markers
Waste yarn for stitch holders

TENSION

12 sts and 17 rounds to 10 cm measured over st st using 7mm (US 10.5/11) needles.

SPECIAL ABBREVIATIONS

MIL (Make 1 left): Insert left-hand needle from front to back under the horizontal strand between last st worked and next st on left-hand needle. Knit into the back loop to twist the stitch— one stitch increased.

MIR (Make 1 right): Insert left-hand needle from back to front under the horizontal strand between last st worked and next st on left-hand needle. Knit into the front loop to twist the stitch—one stitch increased.

PATTERN NOTE

- Jumper is worked in one piece, from neck edge down.
- Neck shaping is worked in rows. After center front sts are cast on, work is joined and completed in the round.
- When yoke is complete, body is joined in one piece and worked in rnds. Sleeves are worked in rnds on double-pointed needles.

YOKE

Using 7mm (US 10.5/11) circular needles, cast on 44 [46: 46: 50: 50] sts.

Row 1 (RS): K1, place marker (PM), K2, PM, K2 [2: 2: 3: 3], PM, K2, PM, K30 [32: 32: 34: 34], PM, K2, PM, K2 [2: 2: 3: 3], PM, K2, PM, K1.

Row 2 and alt rows: Purl.

Row 3: Kfb, MIL, slip marker (SM), K2, SM, MIR, knit to next marker, MIL, SM, K2, SM, MIR, knit to next marker, MIL, SM, K2, SM, MIR, knit to next marker, MIL, SM, K2, SM, MIR, Kfb (10 sts inc). 54 [56: 56: 60: 60] sts.

Row 5: Kfb, knit to next marker, MIL, SM, K2, SM, MIR, knit to next marker, MIL, SM, K2, SM, MIR, knit to next marker, MIL, SM, K2, SM, MIR, knit to next marker, MIL, SM, K2, SM, MIR, knit to last st, Kfb (10 sts inc). 64 [66: 66: 70: 70] sts.

Row 7: Kfb, knit to next marker, MIL, SM, K2, SM, MIR, knit to next marker, MIL, SM, K2, SM, MIR, knit to next marker, MIL, SM, K2, SM, MIR, knit to next marker, MIL, SM, K2, SM, MIR, knit to last st, Kfb (10 sts inc). 74 [76: 76: 80: 80] sts. Turn work and cast on 22 [24: 24: 26: 26] sts for center front. With RS facing, join to beg working in rounds. PM for beg of rnd. 96 [100: 100: 106: 106] sts. Proceed in rounds as follows:

Round 1: Knit.

Round 2: Knit to marker, *MIL, SM, K2, SM, MIR**, knit to next marker, rep from * twice more, then from * to ** once, knit to end of round (8 sts inc). 104 [108: 108: 114: 114] sts.

Round 3: Knit.
Rep last 2 rounds 2 [5: 10: 12: 16] times more. 120 [148: 188: 210: 242] sts.

1st (2nd, 3rd, 4th) sizes only
Next round: Knit to marker, *M1L, SM, K2, SM, M1R**, knit to next marker, rep from * twice more, then from * to ** once, knit to end of round (8 sts inc). 128 [156: 196: 218] sts.
Next round: Knit.
Next round: *Knit to marker, SM, K2, SM, M1R, knit to next marker, M1L, SM, K2, SM, rep from * once more, knit to end (4 sts inc). 132 [160: 200: 222] sts.
Next round: Knit.
Rep last 4 rounds 4 [4: 2: 1] times more. 180 [208: 224: 234] sts.

1st (4th, 5th) sizes only
Next round: Knit to marker, *M1L, SM, K2, SM, M1R**, knit to next marker, rep from * twice more, then from * to ** once, knit to end of round (8 sts inc). 188 [242: 250] sts.
Knit 3 rounds.
Rep last 4 rounds - [- : once] more. 188 [242: 258] sts

All sizes:
Divide for Sleeves and Body:
Next round: Knit to first marker, remove marker, k1. Slip next 38 [42: 44: 47: 49] sts onto scrap yarn for left sleeve, removing the 2 markers. Cast on 4 sts for underarm, placing marker after 2nd st for beg of round. Knit next 56 [62: 68: 74: 80] sts for back, removing the 2 markers. Slip next 38 [42: 44: 47: 49] sts onto scrap yarn for right sleeve, removing the 2 markers. Cast on 4 sts for underarm. Knit last 56 [62: 68: 74: 80] sts for front, removing the raglan marker and original beg of rnd marker. 120 [132: 144: 156: 168] sts for body.

BODY
Knit even in rounds on these 120 [132: 144: 156: 168] sts until body from underarm meas 34.5 [35.5: 35.5: 36.5: 36.5] cm. Change to longer 5mm (US 8) circular needle.
Next round: *K1, P1, rep from * around.
Last row forms rib.
Rep last round 3 times more.
Next round: Knit.
Rep last round 3 times more.
Cast off loosely knitwise.

SLEEVES
Slip 38 [42: 44: 47: 49] sts from scrap yarn onto 7mm (US 10.5/11) double-pointed needles, rejoin yarn and knit across. Pick up and K4 sts along underarm, placing marker after 2nd st for beg of round. Divide sts evenly between 4 needles and join in round. 42 [46: 48: 51: 53] sts.

2nd (3rd, 4th, 5th) sizes only
Knit 14 [10: 10: 8] rounds even.
Next (dec) round: K1, K2tog, knit to last 3 sts, SSK, K1. 44 [46: 49: 51] sts.
Rep dec round every 14th [12th: 12th: 9th] round 1 [2: 2: 3] times more. 42 [42: 45: 45] sts.

All sizes:
Knit even in rounds until sleeve from underarm meas 32 [32: 33: 33: 33] cm.
Begin Wave stitch pattern as folls:
Rounds 1–7: Knit.
Round 8: *[Knit next st together with purl "bump" 7 rounds below] 3 [3: 3: 4: 4] times, K11, rep from * around.
Rounds 9–11: Knit.
Round 12: *K7, [Knit next st together with purl "bump" 7 rounds below] 3 [3: 3: 4: 4] times, K4, rep from * around.
Rounds 13–17: Knit.
Rep rounds 8–17 once more, then rounds 8–12 once.
Next round: K - [- : - : 1: 1] , *K5 [5: 5: 4: 4], K2tog, rep from * 5 [5: 5: 6: 6] times more, K - [- : - : 2: 2]. 36 [36: 36: 38: 38] sts.
Change to 5mm (US 8) double-pointed needles.
Next round: *K1, P1, rep from * around.
Rep last round 3 times more.
Next round: Knit.
Rep last round 3 times more.
Cast off loosely knitwise.

MAKING UP
Press as described on the information page.

COLLAR
With RS facing and 6mm (US 10) circular needle, pick up and K70 [70: 70: 75: 75] sts evenly around neck opening. PM and join to beg working in rounds.
Begin Wave stitch pattern as folls:
Rounds 1–7: Knit.
Round 8: *[Knit next st together with purl "bump" 7 rounds below] 3 [3: 3: 4: 4] times, K11, rep from * around.
Rounds 9–11: Knit.
Round 12: *K7, [Knit next st together with purl "bump" 7 rounds below] 3 [3: 3: 4: 4] times, K4, rep from * around.
Rounds 13–17: Knit.
Rep rounds 8–17 once more, then rounds 8–12 once.
Next round: Knit, decreasing - [- : - : 1: 1] st at center of round. 70 [70: 70: 74: 74] sts.
Change to shorter 5mm (US 8) circular needles.
Next round: *K1, P1, rep from * around.
Rep last round 3 times more.
Next round: Knit.
Rep last round 3 times more.
Cast off loosely knitwise.

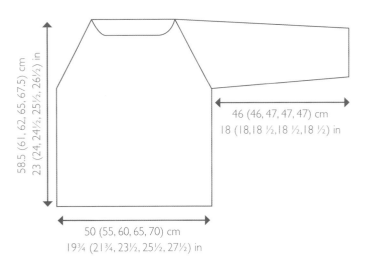

58.5 (61, 62, 65, 67.5) cm
23 (24, 24½, 25½, 26½) in

46 (46, 47, 47, 47) cm
18 (18,18 ½,18 ½,18 ½) in

50 (55, 60, 65, 70) cm
19¾ (21¾, 23½, 25½, 27½) in

COCOON ••

SIZE

To fit bust	81-86	91-97	102-107	112-117	122-127	cm
	32-34	36-38	40-42	44-46	48-50	in
Actual bust measurement of garment						
	92	114.5	136.5	159	181	cm
	36¼	45	53¾	62½	71¼	in

YARN

Rowan Big Wool (photographed in Glum 056)

	11	12	13	14	15	100gm

NEEDLES

10mm (no 000) (US 15) circular needle, 100-120cm in length
10mm (no 000) (US15) double pointed needles

EXTRAS

Waste yarn
Removable stitch markers

TENSION

9 sts and 14 rows to 10 cm measured over Moss stitch using 10mm (US 15) needles.
12 sts and 15 rows to 10 cm measured over K1, P1 rib using 10mm (US 15) needles.

PATTERN NOTE

Body is worked flat but a circular needle is recommended to accommodate the number of sts. Body Edging, Cuff Edging and Pockets are worked in the round.

BODY

Using 10mm (US 15) circular needle, cast on 83 [103: 123: 143: 163] sts. Do not join, work back and forth in rows.
Next row: K1, *P1, K1, rep from * to end.
This row forms moss st.
Work in moss stitch until work meas 10 cm, ending with RS facing for next row.
Add pocket openings
Next row (RS): Patt 6 [8: 12: 15: 19] sts, K next 11 sts with waste yarn, slide these sts back to LH needle and K these sts with working yarn, cont in patt as set to last 17 [19: 23: 26: 30] sts, K next 11 sts with waste yarn, slide these sts back to LH needle and K these sts with working yarn, patt to end.
Next row (WS): Patt to end in moss st as set.
Cont straight in moss st until work meas 25 [27.5: 30: 32.5: 35] cm, ending with RS facing for next row.

Shape cuff opening

Cast off 3 [4: 5: 5: 6] sts at beg of next 2 rows. 77 [95: 113: 133: 151] sts.
Cont straight in patt as set until work meas 35 [37.5: 40: 42.5: 45] cm, ending with RS facing for next row.
Cast on 3 [4: 5: 5: 6] sts at beg of next 2 rows, incorporating new sts into moss st as set. 83 [103: 123: 143: 163] sts.
Patt straight until work meas 60 [65: 70: 75: 80] cm, ending with RS facing for next row.
Cast off in patt.

MAKING UP

Press as described on the information page.
Fold Body lengthwise to match cast-on edge with cast-off edge; these edges remain open for the Body Edging. Join side edges of row-ends from cast-on/cast-off edge to cuff opening. Rep for other side. Open garment to shape.

BODY EDGING

With RS facing and using 10mm (US 15) circular needle, starting at right side seam, pick up and knit 110 [137: 164: 190: 217] sts evenly along cast-off edge to left side seam, then pick up and knit 110 [137: 164: 190: 217] sts evenly along cast-on edge. Join to work in the round and place marker for beg of round.
Rib Round: *K1, P1, rep from * to end.
This round forms rib.
Work in rib until edging meas 7cm.
Cast off loosely in rib.

CUFF EDGING

With RS facing and using 10mm (US 15) double pointed needles, pick up and knit 24 sts evenly around cuff opening. Join to work in the round and place marker for beg of round. 24 sts.
Work in rib as for body edging for 7 cm.
Cast off loosely in rib.

POCKETS (both alike)

With RS facing and using 10mm (US 15) double pointed needles, carefully unpick the waste yarn from the pocket opening, placing 11 sts from top of opening and 11 sts from bottom of opening onto double pointed needles. 22 sts.
Rejoin yarn and knit to end. Join to work in the round and place marker for beg of round.
Work in st st (knit every rnd) until pocket meas 9 cm.
Push pocket through to WS of garment and work a 3-needle cast off from inside to close bottom seam. Sew to cast-on edge of ribbed neckline to secure.

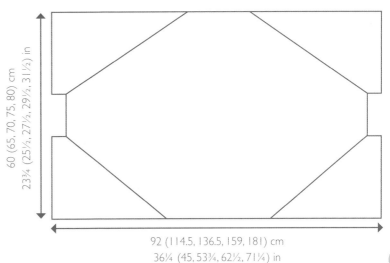

60 (65, 70, 75, 80) cm
23¾ (25½, 27½, 29½, 31½) in

92 (114.5, 136.5, 159, 181) cm
36¼ (45, 53¾, 62½, 71¼) in

SWERVE SCARF ••

SIZE
25.5cm/10in wide and 203cm/80in long

YARN
Rowan Big Wool (photographed in shade Normandy 086)
6 × 100gm

NEEDLES
8mm (no 0) (US 11) needles

TENSION
6.5 sts and 20 rows to 10cm / 4in over brioche stitch using 8mm
(US 11) needles once blocked

SPECIAL ABBREVIATIONS

BK3tog / right leaning decrease: K3tog (the next knit
stitch with its paired yarn over and the following purl stitch), slip
the resulting stitch back to the left needle, pass the following
2 stitches (a knit stitch and its paired yarn over) over the first
stitch on the left needle and off the left needle, move the
resulting stitch back to the right needle. [2 stitches decreased]

BSK2P / left leaning decrease: Slip 1 brioche stitch with
its paired yarn over together knitwise, k3tog (the next purl
stitch with the following knit stitch and its paired yarn over),
pass the slip stitch and its paired yarn over together over and
off the right needle.

BK2tog-yo-BK2tog / symmetrical increase: brioche
knit 2 together (the next stitch with its paired yarn over)
without slipping stitch off left needle; yarn over on right needle;
brioche knit 2 together (the same stitch with its paired yarn
over once again) and drop resulting stitch off left needle. *Note:
on the following row, increased stitches need to be worked as (yo, sl,
k1) rather than (yo, sl, K2tog).*

SCARF
Using 8mm (US 11) needles cast on 24 sts.
Row 1 (set up row): *Yo, sl, K1, rep from * to end.
Rows 2-8: *Yo, sl, K2tog, rep from * to end *[basic brioche]*.
Row 9: [Yo, sl, K2tog] 9 times, yo, sl, BK3tog, yo, sl, BK2tog-
yo-BK2tog.
Row 10: Yo, sl, K1, *yo, sl, K2tog, rep from * to end.
Work 2 rows in basic brioche.
Row 13: [Yo, sl, K2tog] 8 times, yo, sl, BK3tog, yo, sl,
BK2tog-yo-BK2tog, yo, sl, K2tog.
Row 14: Yo, sl, K2tog, yo, sl, K1, *yo, sl, K2tog, rep
from * to end.
Work 2 rows in basic brioche.
Row 17: [Yo, sl, K2tog] 7 times, yo, sl, BK3tog, yo, sl,
BK2tog-yo-BK2tog, [yo, sl, K2tog] twice.
Row 18: [Yo, sl, K2tog] twice, yo, sl, K1, *yo, sl, K2tog,
rep from * to end.
Work 2 rows in basic brioche.
Row 21: [Yo, sl, K2tog] 6 times, yo, sl, BK3tog, yo, sl,
BK2tog-yo-BK2tog, [yo, sl, K2tog] 3 times.
Row 22: [Yo, sl, K2tog] 3 times, yo, sl, K1, *yo, sl, K2tog,
rep from * to end.
Work 2 rows in basic brioche.
Row 25: [Yo, sl, K2tog] 5 times, yo, sl, BK3tog, yo, sl,
BK2tog-yo-BK2tog, [yo, sl, K2tog] 4 times.
Row 26: [Yo, sl, K2tog] 4 times, yo, sl, k1, *yo, sl, K2tog,
rep from * to end.
Work 2 rows in basic brioche.

Row 29: [Yo, sl, K2tog] 4 times, yo, sl, BK3tog, yo, sl, BK2tog-yo-BK2tog, [yo, sl, K2tog] 5 times.
Row 30: [Yo, sl, K2tog] 5 times, yo, sl, k1, *yo, sl, K2tog, rep from * to end.
Work 2 rows in basic brioche.
Row 33: [Yo, sl, K2tog] 3 times, yo, sl, BK3tog, yo, sl, BK2tog-yo-BK2tog, [yo, sl, K2tog] 6 times.
Row 34: [Yo, sl, K2tog] 6 times, yo, sl, k1, *yo, sl, K2tog, rep from * to end.
Work 2 rows in basic brioche.
Row 37: [Yo, sl, K2tog] twice, yo, sl, BK3tog, yo, sl, BK2tog-yo-BK2tog, [yo, sl, K2tog] 7 times.
Row 38: [Yo, sl, K2tog] 7 times, yo, sl, k1, *yo, sl, K2tog, rep from * to end.
Work 2 rows in basic brioche.
Row 41: Yo, sl, K2tog, yo, sl, BK3tog, yo, sl, BK2tog-yo-BK2tog, [yo, sl, K2tog] 8 times.
Row 42: [Yo, sl, K2tog] 8 times, yo, sl, k1, *yo, sl, K2tog, rep from * to end.
Work 2 rows in basic brioche.
Row 45: Yo, sl, BK3tog, yo, sl, BK2tog-yo-BK2tog, [yo, sl, K2tog] 9 times.
Row 46: [Yo, sl, K2tog] 9 times, yo, sl, k1, *yo, sl, K2tog, rep from * to end.
Work 2 rows in basic brioche.
Row 49: Yo, sl, BK2tog-yo-BK2tog, yo, sl, BSK2P, [yo, sl, K2tog] 9 times.
Row 50: [Yo, sl, K2tog] 10 times, yo, sl, k1, yo, sl, K2tog.
Work 2 rows in basic brioche.
Row 53: Yo, sl, K2tog, yo, sl, BK2tog-yo-BK2tog, yo, sl, BSK2P, [yo, sl, K2tog] 8 times.
Row 54: [Yo, sl, K2tog] 8 times, yo, sl, k1, *yo, sl, K2tog, rep from * to end.
Work 2 rows in basic brioche.
Row 57: [Yo, sl, K2tog] twice, yo, sl, BK2tog-yo-BK2tog, yo, sl, BSK2P, [yo, sl, K2tog] 7 times.
Row 58: [Yo, sl, K2tog] 7 times, yo, sl, k1, *yo, sl, K2tog, rep from * to end.
Work 2 rows in basic brioche.
Row 61: [Yo, sl, K2tog] 3 times, yo, sl, BK2tog-yo-BK2tog, yo, sl, BSK2P, [yo, sl, K2tog] 6 times.
Row 62: [Yo, sl, K2tog] 6 times, yo, sl, k1, *yo, sl, K2tog, rep from * to end.
Work 2 rows in basic brioche.
Row 65: [Yo, sl, K2tog] 4 times, yo, sl, BK2tog-yo-BK2tog, yo, sl, BSK2P, [yo, sl, K2tog] 5 times.
Row 66: [Yo, sl, K2tog] 5 times, yo, sl, k1, *yo, sl, K2tog, rep from * to end.
Work 2 rows in basic brioche.
Row 69: [Yo, sl, K2tog] 5 times, yo, sl, BK2tog-yo-BK2tog, yo, sl, BSK2P, [yo, sl, K2tog] 4 times.
Row 70: [Yo, sl, K2tog] 4 times, yo, sl, k1, *yo, sl, K2tog, rep from * to end..
Work 2 rows in basic brioche.
Row 73: [Yo, sl, K2tog] 6 times, yo, sl, BK2tog-yo-BK2tog, yo, sl, BSK2P, [yo, sl, K2tog] 3 times.
Row 74: [Yo, sl, K2tog] 3 times, yo, sl, k1, *yo, sl, K2tog, rep from * to end.
Work 2 rows in basic brioche.
Row 77: [Yo, sl, K2tog] 7 times, yo, sl, BK2tog-yo-BK2tog, yo, sl, BSK2P, [yo, sl, K2tog] twice.

Row 78: [Yo, sl, K2tog] twice, yo, sl, k1, *yo, sl, K2tog, rep from * to end.
Work 2 rows in basic brioche.
Row 81: [Yo, sl, K2tog] 8 times, yo, sl, BK2tog-yo-BK2tog, yo, sl, BSK2P, yo, sl, K2tog.
Row 82: Yo, sl, K2tog, yo, sl, k1, *yo, sl, K2tog, rep from * to end.
Work 2 rows in basic brioche.
Row 85: [Yo, sl, K2tog] 9 times, yo, sl, BK2tog-yo-BK2tog, yo, sl, BSK2P.
Row 86: Yo, sl, k1, *yo, sl, K2tog, rep from * to end.
Work 6 rows in basic brioche.
Repeat from row 9, four times more.
Work a further 2 rows in basic brioche.
Cast off: P1, (K2tog, pass stitch over, P1, pass stitch over) to last 2 sts, K2tog, pass stitch over, break yarn and fasten off.

SWERVE BEANIE •

SIZE
To fit average sized woman's head

YARN
Rowan Big Wool
2 x 100gm
(photographed in Normandy 086)

NEEDLES
7mm (no 2) (US 10.5) double pointed needles

TENSION
10.5 sts and 24 rows to 10cm / 4in worked over brioche stitch (unblocked)

SPECIAL ABBREVIATIONS
BK3tog / right leaning decrease: K3tog (the next knit stitch with its paired yarn over and the following purl stitch), slip the resulting stitch back to the left needle, pass the following 2 stitches (a knit stitch and its paired yarn over) over the first stitch on the left needle and off the left needle, move the resulting stitch back to the right needle.
[2 stitches decreased]
BK2tog-yo-BK2tog / symmetrical increase: brioche knit 2 together (the next stitch with its paired yarn over) without slipping stitch off left needle; yarn over on right needle; brioche knit 2 together (the same stitch with its paired yarn over once again) and drop resulting stitch off left needle.
Note: on the following row, increased stitches need to be worked as (yo, sl, k1) rather than (yo, sl, k2tog).

HAT
Using 7mm (US 10.5) double pointed needles, cast on 50 sts. Divide sts evenly over 4 needles (16 [17: 17] sts on each needle). Place a marker (for start of rnd) and join in round, being careful not to twist sts.
Round 1 (set up round): *K1, yo, sl, rep from * around. (Yarn overs are 'paired' with their brioche knit stitch so don't count as increased stitches.)
Round 2: *Yo, sl, P2tog, rep from * around. *[basic brioche purl round].*
Round 3: *K2tog, yo, sl, rep from * around *[basic brioche knit round].*
Repeat rounds 2 and 3 once more, then round 2 once again.
Round 7: *[K2tog, yo, sl] twice, BK3tog, yo, sl, BK2tog-yo-BK2tog, yo, sl, rep from * 4 times more.

Round 8: *[Yo, sl, P2tog] 3 times, yo, sl, P1, yo, sl, P2tog, rep from * 4 times more.
Round 9: As round 3.
Round 10: As round 2.
Round 11: *K2tog, yo, sl, BK3tog, yo, sl, BK2tog-yo-BK2tog, yo, sl, K2tog, yo, sl, rep from * 4 times more.
Round 12: *[Yo, sl, P2tog] twice, yo, sl, P1, [yo, sl, P2tog] twice, rep from * 4 times more.
Round 13: As round 3.
Round 14: As round 2.
Round 15: *BK3tog, yo, sl, BK2tog-yo-BK2tog, yo, sl, [K2tog, yo, sl] twice, rep from * 4 times more.
Round 16: *Yo, sl, P2tog, yo, sl, P1, [yo, sl, P2tog] 3 times, rep from * 4 times more.
Beg with a purl round, work in basic brioche (alternating purl and knit rounds) until work measures 18 cm from cast-on edge, ending with a brioche purl round.
Next round: *[K2tog, yo, sl] 3 times, BK3tog, yo, sl, rep from * 4 times more. 40 sts (not counting yarn overs).
Beg with a purl round, work 3 rounds in basic brioche.
Next round: *[K2tog, yo, sl] twice, BK3tog, yo, sl, rep from * 4 times more. 30 sts (not counting yarn overs).
Beg with a purl round, work 3 rounds in basic brioche.
Next round: *K2tog, yo, sl, BK3tog, yo, sl, rep from * 4 times more. 20 sts (not counting yarn overs).
Beg with a purl round, work 3 rounds in basic brioche.
Next round: *BK3tog, yo, sl, rep from * 4 times more. 10 sts (not counting yarn overs).
Next round: *K1, p2tog, rep from * around. 10 sts.

Break yarn and thread onto a tapestry needle, draw yarn through remaining 10 sts, pull taught and bring yarn end through to the inside. Weave in all ends and block.

INFORMATION

TENSION

Obtaining the correct tension is perhaps the single factor which can make the difference between a successful garment and a disastrous one. It controls both the shape and size of an article, so any variation, however slight, can distort the finished garment. Different designers feature in our books and it is their tension, given at the start of each pattern, which you must match. We recommend that you knit a square in pattern and/or stocking stitch (depending on the pattern instructions) of perhaps 5 - 10 more stitches and 5 - 10 more rows than those given in the tension note. Mark out the central 10cm square with pins. If you have too many stitches to 10cm try again using thicker needles, if you have too few stitches to 10cm try again using finer needles. Once you have achieved the correct tension your garment will be knitted to the measurements indicated in the size diagram shown at the end of the pattern.

CHART NOTE

When following a chart, each square represents an instruction and each line of squares is a row of knitting. Each colour used is given a different letter and these are shown in the materials section, or in the key alongside the chart of each pattern. When working from the charts, read odd rows (K) from right to left and even rows (P) from left to right, unless otherwise stated. When working lace from a chart it is important to note that all but the largest size may have to alter the first and last few stitches in order not to lose or gain stitches over the row.

WORKING A LACE PATTERN

When working a lace pattern it is important to remember that if you are unable to work both the increase and corresponding decrease and vice versa, the stitches should be worked in stocking stitch.

KNITTING WITH COLOUR

There are two main methods of working colour into a knitted fabric: Intarsia and Fairisle techniques. The first method produces a single thickness of fabric and is usually used where a colour is only required in a particular area of a row and does not form a repeating pattern across the row, as in the fairisle technique.

Fairisle type knitting: When two or three colours are worked repeatedly across a row, strand the yarn not in use loosely behind the stitches being worked. If you are working with more than two colours, treat the "floating" yarns as if they were one yarn and always spread the stitches to their correct width to keep them elastic. It is advisable not to carry the stranded or "floating" yarns over more than three stitches at a time, but to weave them under and over the colour you are working. The "floating" yarns are therefore caught at the back of the work.

Intarsia: The simplest way to do this is to cut short lengths of yarn for each motif or block of colour used in a row. Then joining in the various colours at the appropriate point on the row, link one colour to the next by twisting them around each other where they meet on the wrong side to avoid gaps. All ends can then either be darned along the colour join lines, as each motif is completed or then can be "knitted-in" to the fabric of the knitting as each colour is worked into the pattern. This is done in much the same way as "weaving- in" yarns when working the Fairisle technique and does save time darning-in ends. It is essential that the tension is noted for intarsia as this may vary from the stocking stitch if both are used in the same pattern.

After working for hours knitting a garment, it seems a great pity that many garments are spoiled because such little care is taken in the pressing and finishing process. Follow the text below for a truly professional-looking garment.

Block out each piece of knitting and following the instructions on the ball band press the garment pieces, omitting the ribs. Tip: Take special care to press the edges, as this will make sewing up both easier and neater. If the ball band indicates that the fabric is not to be pressed, then covering the blocked out fabric with a damp white cotton cloth and leaving it to stand will have the desired effect. Darn in all ends neatly along the selvage edge or a colour join, as appropriate.

STITCHING

When stitching the pieces together, remember to match areas of colour and texture very carefully where they meet. Use a seam stitch such as back stitch or mattress stitch for all main knitting seams and join all ribs and neckband with mattress stitch unless otherwise stated.

CONSTRUCTION

Having completed the pattern instructions, join left shoulder and neckband seams as detailed above. Sew the top of the sleeve to the body of the garment using the method detailed in the pattern referring to the appropriate guide:

Straight cast-off sleeves: Place centre of cast-off edge of sleeve to shoulder seam. Sew top of sleeve to body, using markers as guidelines where applicable.

Square set-in sleeves: Place centre of cast-off edge of sleeve to shoulder seam. Set sleeve head into armhole, the straight sides at top of sleeve to form a neat right-angle to cast-off sts at armhole of back and front.

Shallow set-in sleeves: Place centre of cast off edge of sleeve to shoulder seam. Match decreases at beg of armhole shaping to decreases at top of sleeve. Sew sleeve head into armhole, easing in shapings.

Set-in sleeves: Place centre of cast-off edge of sleeve to shoulder seam. Set sleeve, easing sleeve head into armhole. Join side and sleeve seams.

Slip stitch pocket edgings and linings into place. Sew on buttons to correspond with buttonholes. Ribbed welts and neckbands and any areas garter stitch should not be pressed.

ABBREVIATIONS

	knit
	purl
(s)	stitch(es)
	increas(e)(ing)
c	decreas(e)(ing)
st	stocking stitch (I row K, I row P)
t	garter stitch (K every row)
g	begin(ning)
l	following
m	remain(ing)
v st st	reverse stocking stitch
	(I row K , I row P)
p	repeat
	alternate
nt	continue
tt	pattern
g	together
m	millimetres
	centimetres
(s)	inch(es)
	right side
S	wrong side
	slip one stitch
so	pass slipped stitch over
sso	pass 2 slipped stitches over
	through back of loop
	make one stitch by picking up
	horizontal loop before next stitch
	and knitting into back of it
IP	make one stitch by picking up
	horizontal loop before next stitch
	and purlinginto back of it
wd	yarn forward
n	yarn round needle
eas	measures
	no stitches, times or rows
	no stitches, times or rows for
	that size
	yarn over needle
n	yarn forward round needle
ib	with yarn at back
togK	slip 2 stitches together
	knitways

EXPERIENCE RATING

(For guidance only)

• Beginner Techniques

For the beginner knitter, basic garment shaping and straight forward stitch technique.

• • Simple Techniques

Simple straight forward knitting, introducing various, shaping techniques and garments.

• • • Experienced Techniques

For the more experienced knitter, using more advanced shaping techniques at the same time as colourwork or more advanced stitch techniques.

• • • • Advanced Techniques

Advanced techniques used, using advanced stitches and garment shapings and more challenging techniques

BUTTONS & RIBBON

Groves & Banks
Eastern Bypass
Thame
Oxfordshire
OX9 3FU
www.grovesltd.co.uk
groves@stockistenquiries.co.uk

Bedecked Haberdashery
The Coach House
Barningham Park
RICHMOND
DL11 7DW
Tel: +44 (0)1833 621 451
eMail:Judith.lewis@bedecked.co.uk
www.bedecked.co.uk

WASH CARE INFORMATION

You may have noticed over the last season that the wash care symbols on our ball bands and shade cards have changed. This is to bring the symbols we use up to date and hopefully help you to care for your knitting and crochet more easily. Below are the symbols you are likely to see and a brief explanation of each.

MACHINE WASH SYMBOLS

HAND WASH SYMBOLS

DRY CLEAN SYMBOLS

IRONING SYMBOLS

DO NOT BLEACH SYMBOL

DRYING SYMBOLS

SIZING GUIDE

When you knit and wear a Rowan design we want you to look and feel fabulous. This all starts with the size and fit of the design you choose. To help you to achieve a great knitting experience we have looked at the sizing of our womens and menswear patterns. This has resulted in the introduction of our new sizing guide which includes the following exciting features:

Our sizing now conforms to standard clothing sizes. Therefore if you buy a standard size 12 in clothing, then our medium patterns will fit you perfectly.

The menswear designs are now available to knit in menswear si XSmall through to 2XL ie. 38" to 50" chest.

We have now added a UNISEX sizing guide. This is the SAME as t Mens standard sizing guide with an XXSmall size being added.

Dimensions in the charts below are body measurements, not garme dimensions, therefore please refer to the measuring guide to help y to determine which is the best size for you to knit.

STANDARD WOMENS SIZING GUIDE

The sizing within this chart is also based on the larger size within the range, ie. M will be based on size 14.

UK SIZE DUAL SIZE	S 8/10	M 12/14	L 16/18	XL 20/22	XXL 24/26	
To fit bust	32 – 34	36 – 38	40 – 42	44 – 46	48 – 50	inches
	81 – 86	91 - 97	102 – 107	112 – 117	122 – 127	cm
To fit waist	24 – 26	28 – 30	32 – 34	36 – 38	40 – 42	inches
	61 – 66	71 – 76	81 – 86	91 – 97	102 – 107	cm
To fit hips	34 – 36	38 – 40	42 – 44	46 – 48	50 – 52	inches
	86 – 91	97 – 102	107 – 112	117 – 122	127 – 132	cm

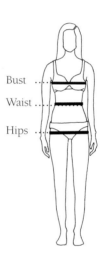

Bust ......
Waist ......
Hips ......

STANDARD MENS AND UNISEX SIZING GUIDE

Mens sizes: XS to 2XL. Unisex Sizes: XXS to 2XL

UK SIZE EUR Size	XXS 46	XS 48	S 50	M 52	L 54	XL 56	XXL 58	2XL 60	
To fit chest	36	38	40	42	44	46	48	50	inches
	91	97	102	107	112	117	122	127	cm
To fit waist	28	30	32	34	36	38	40	42	inches
	71	76	81	86	91	97	102	107	cm

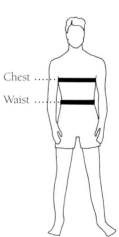

Chest ......
Waist ......

MEASURING GUIDE

For maximum comfort and to ensure the correct fit when choosing a size to knit, please follow the tips below when checking your size.

Measure yourself close to your body, over your underwear and don't pull the tape measure too tight!

Bust/chest – measure around the fullest part of the bust/chest and across the shoulder blades.

Waist – measure around the natural waistline, just above the hip bone.

Hips – measure around the fullest part of the bottom.

If you don't wish to measure yourself, note the size of a favourite jumper that you like the fit of. Our sizes are now comparable to the clothing sizes from the major high street retailers, so if your favourite jumper is a size Medium or size 12, then our size Medium should be approximately the same fit.

To be extra sure, measure your favourite jumper and then compare these measurements with the Rowan size diagram given at the end of the individual instructions.

Finally, once you have decided which size is best for you, please ensure that you achieve the tension required for the design you wish to knit. Remember if your tension is too loose, your garment will be bigger than the pattern size and you may use more yarn. If your tension is too tight, your garment could be smaller than the pattern size and you will have yarn left over.

Furthermore if your tension is incorrect, the handle of your fabric will be too stiff or floppy and will not fit properly. It really does make sense to check your tension before starting every project.

MODEL SIZE INFORMATION

Model wears a UK dress size 8, height 5ft 7in.

All of the photography garments were knitted in the following bust size: 32-34in

SIZING & SIZE DIAGRAM NOTE

The instructions are given for the smallest size. Where they vary, work the figures in brackets for the larger sizes. One set of figures refers to all sizes. Included with most patterns in this magazine is a 'size diagram' - see image on the right, of the finished garment and its dimensions. The measurement shown at the bottom of each 'size diagram' shows the garment width 2.5cm below the armhole

shaping. To help you choose the size of garment to knit please refer to the sizing guide. Generally in the majority of designs the welt width (at the cast on edge of the garment) is the same width as the chest. However, some designs are 'A-Line' in shape or have a flared edge and in these cases the welt width will be wider than the chest width.

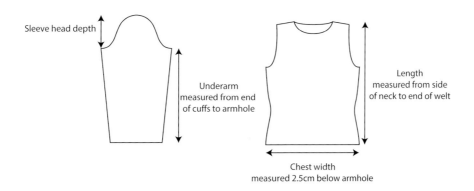

Sleeve head depth

Underarm measured from end of cuffs to armhole

Length measured from side of neck to end of welt

Chest width measured 2.5cm below armhole

LOLA ●●●

GRÖSSEN

Passend für Oberweite

81-86	91-97	102-107	112-117	122-127	cm

Gestrickte Oberweite

90	100	110	120	130	cm

GARN

A Rowan Alpaca Classic (fotografiert in Dusk 130)

8	9	9	10	11	x 25g balls

B Rowan Kidsilk Haze (fotografiert in Shadow 653)

4	5	5	6	6	x 25g balls

NADELN

2 Rundstrickndl Nr. 3,25, 40 cm lang
1 Nadelspiel Nr. 3,25
1 Rundstrickndl Nr. 3,5, 80 cm lang
Je 1 Rundstrickndl Nr. 4, 40 und 80 cm lang
1 Nadelspiel Nr. 4

EXTRAS

Hilfsnadeln
Maschenmarkierer (Mm)
Fremdgarn für den offenen Anschlag

MASCHENPROBE

20 M und 24 Runden = 10 x 10 cm, glatt re gestr mit Ndl Nr. 4
und je einem Fd in Fbe A und B zus gestr.

SPEZIELLE ABKÜRZUNGEN

LiZun = Mit der li Ndl den Querfaden zwischen beiden Nadeln
von vorne nach hinten aufnehmen und re str, dabei von hinten in
die Schlinge einstechen.
ReZun = Mit der li Ndl den Querfaden zwischen beiden
Nadeln von hinten nach vorne aufnehmen und re str, dabei von
vorne in die Schlinge einstechen.
Mmabh = Den Mm auf die re Ndl heben.

HINWEISE

Der Pullover wird in einem Stück von oben nach unten gestr.

HALSBLENDE

112 (120: 124: 128: 132) M mit der Rundstrickndl Nr. 3,25 und
dem Fremdgarn anschl.
In Runden str wie folgt, dabei beachten, dass in der 1. Rde die M
nicht verdreht sind, Anf und Ende jeder Rde markieren:
Rde 1: Re.
Diese Rde noch 1 x wdhl.
Den Fd abschneiden, mit Fbe A und B zus wie folgt str:
Rde 1 (Hinr): *1 M re, 1 M li, ab * wdhl bis zum Ende.
Weiter im Rippenmuster str bis 4 cm erreicht sind.
Nächste Rde: Li (für die Bruchlinie).
Nächste Rde: *1 M re, 1 M li, ab * wdhl bis zum Ende.
Weiter im Rippenmuster str bis 4 cm erreicht sind.
Den Fremdfaden an der Anschlagkante vorsichtig entfernen, die
offenen M auf eine Hilfsndl Nr. 3,25 heben, die Halsblende in
der Hälfte nach innen umlegen, die M wie folgt verbinden:

Nächste Rde: *Die nächste M auf der Ndl mit der nächsten
M der Anschlagkante re zus-str, ab * wdhl bis zum Ende der Rde
= 112 (120: 124: 128: 132) M.

PASSE

Wechseln zur kurzen Rundstrickndl Nr. 4.
Basis-R: *1 M re, einen Mm auf die re Ndl, 36 (40: 42: 44: 46) M re,
einen Mm auf die re Ndl, 1 M re, einen Mm auf die re Ndl, 18 M re,
einen Mm auf die re Ndl, ab * noch 1 x wdhl.
Rde 1: *1 M re, Mmabh, LiZun, re bis zum nächsten Mm,
ReZun, Mmabh, 1 M re, Mmabh, LiZun, re bis zum nächsten
Mm, ReZun, Mmabh, ab * noch 1 x wdhl = 8 Zun = 120 (128:
132: 136: 140) M.
Rde 2: Re.
Die beiden letzten Runden 22 (23: 21: 22: 21) x wdhl, wechseln
zur langen Rundstrickndl, wenn nicht mehr alle M auf die Ndl
passen = 296 (312: 300: 312: 308) M.
Größe 2, 3 und 4 speziell
Nächste Rde: 1 M re, Mmabh, LiZun, re bis zum nächsten
Mm, ReZun, Mmabh, 1 M re, Mmabh, LiZun, re bis zum
nächsten Mm, ReZun, Mmabh, ab * noch 1 x wdhl = 8 Zun =
308 (320: 316) M.
Nächste Rde 2: Re.
Nächste Rde: *1 M re, Mmabh, LiZun, re bis zum nächsten
Mm, ReZun, Mmabh, 1 M re, Mmabh, re bis zum nächsten Mm,
Mmabh, 1 M re, Mmabh, ReZun, ab * noch 1 x wdhl = 4 Zun =
312 (324: 320) M.
Nächste Rde: Re.
Die letzten 4 Runden 1 (2: 4) x wdhl = 324 (348: 368) M.
Alle Größen
Alle Mm entfernen.
Armausschnitte

Nächste Rde: 84 (90: 96: 104: 112) M re (für das Rückenteil), die nächsten 64 (66: 66: 70: 72) M für den li Ärmel auf einer Hilfsndl stilllegen, 6 (10: 14: 16: 18) M anschl (für den Armausschnitt), die nächsten 84 (90: 96: 104: 112) M re str für das Vorderteil, die nächsten 64 (66: 66: 70: 72) M für den re Ärmel auf einer 2. Hilfsndl stilllegen, 6 (10: 14: 16: 18) M anschl, dabei nach der 3. (5.: 7.: 8.: 9.) Anschlagmasche einen Mm auf die re Ndl hängen (für Anf und Ende der Rde) = 180 (200: 220: 240: 260) M.

BODY

In Runden glatt re weiterstr bis 26 (26: 27: 28: 28) cm ab den Armausschnitten erreicht ist.
Wechseln zur Rundstrickndl Nr. 3,5.
Nächste Rde: *1 M re, 1 M li, ab * wdhl bis zum Ende.
Weiter im Rippenmuster str bis 5 cm erreicht sind, danach alle M locker abk.

ÄRMEL

Die 64 (66: 66: 70: 72) M eines Ärmels auf das Nadelspiel nehmen, aus den Anschlagmaschen für den Armausschnitt 6 (10: 14: 16: 18) M aufn und re str, dabei nach der 3. (5.: 7.: 8.: 9.) M einen Mm auf die re Ndl hängen (für Anf und Ende der Rde).
Die 70 (76: 80: 86: 90) M gleichmäßig auf 4 Nadeln verteilen und in Runden glatt re str bis 34 (34: 35,5: 35,5: 35,5) cm erreicht sind.
Nächste Rde: 17 (19: 20: 21: 22) x (2 M re zus-str), 2 (-: -: 2: 2) M re, 17 (19: 20: 21: 22) x (2 M re zus-str) = 36 (38: 40: 44: 46) M.
Wechseln zum Nadelspiel Nr. 3,25.
Nächste Rde: *1 M re, 1 M li, ab * wdhl bis zum Ende.
Weiter im Rippenmuster str bis 10 cm erreicht sind.
Nächste Rde: Li (für die Bruchfalte).
Nächste Rde: *1 M re, 1 M li, ab * wdhl bis zum Ende.
Weiter im Rippenmuster str bis weitere 10 cm erreicht sind.
Alle M locker im Muster abk.

FERTIGSTELLUNG

Alle Teile dämpfen, siehe Informationsseite.
Das Bündchen nach innen umlegen und festnähen.

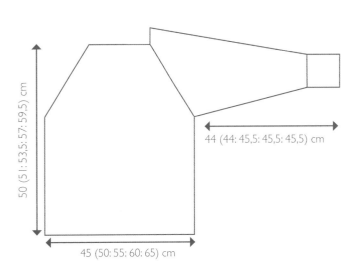

50 (51: 53,5: 57: 59,5) cm

44 (44: 45,5: 45,5: 45,5) cm

45 (50: 55: 60: 65) cm

DIMPLE ●●

GRÖSSE
Passend für eine durchschnittliche Kopfgröße

GARN
Rowan Alpaca Classic
2 x 25 g
(fotografiert in Soft Satin 116

Rowan Kidsilk Haze
1 x 25 g
(fotografiert in White 612)

NADELN
1 Nadelspiel Nr. 3,75

MASCHENPROBE
23 M und 31 R = 10 x 10 cm, glatt re gestr mit Alpaca Classic und Ndl Nr. 3,75

SPEZIELLE ABKÜRZUNGEN
Noppe = (1 M re, 1 M li, 1 M re, 1 M li, 1 M re) locker in die nächste M, danach mit der li Ndl die 2., 3., 4. und 5. M auf der re Ndl einzeln über die 1. M ziehen.
2übzAbn = 2 M re zus abheben, 1 M re, die beiden abgeh M überziehen.

MÜTZE
100 M mit dem Nadelspiel Nr. 3,75 und je einem Fd in Alpaca Classic und 2 Fäden in Kidsilk Haze zus anschl.
Die M gleichmäßig auf den Nadeln verteilen, in Runden str wie folgt, dabei beachten, dass in der 1. Rde die M nicht verdreht sind, Anf und Ende jeder Rde markieren:
Rde 1: *1 M re, 1 M li, ab * wdhl bis zum Ende.
Diese Rde 13 x wdhl, dabei in der letzten Rde gleichmäßig 4 M zun = 104 M.
Nächste Rde: Re.
Die beiden Fäden in Kidsilk Haze abschneiden, nur noch mit Alpaca Classic str wie folgt:
16 Runden re str, danach im Muster str wie folgt:

Rde 1: (Noppe, 7 M re) wdhl bis zum Ende.
Rde 2-4: Re.
Rde 5: (4 M re, Noppe, 3 M re) wdhl bis zum Ende.
Rde 6-8: Re.
Rde 1-8 noch 4 x wdhl = 5 Rapporte insgesamt und 40 Runden im Muster.
Nächste Rde: (Noppe, 3 M re, 2übzAbn, 1 M re) wdhl bis zum Ende = 78 M.
3 Runden re str.
Nächste Rde: (2 M re, Noppe, 2übzAbn) wdhl bis zum Ende = 52 M.
3 Runden re str.
Nächste Rde: (Noppe, 2übzAbn) wdhl bis zum Ende = 26 M.
Nächste Rde: (2 M re zus-str) wdhl bis zum Ende = 13 M.
Nächste rde: 1 M re, (2 M re zus-str) wdhl bis zum Ende = 7 M.
Den Fd abschneiden und durch die restl M ziehen, die M fest zusammenziehen, den Fd gut vernähen.

FERTIGSTELLUNG
Die Mütze dämpfen, siehe Informationsseite.

DARCY ●●

GRÖSSEN

Passend für Oberweite

81-86	91-97	102-107	112-117	122-127	cm

Gestrickte Oberweite

88	98	108	118	128	cm

GARN

A Rowan Alpaca Classic (fotografiert in Snowflake White 111)

11	12	12	13	14	x 25g

B Rowan Kidsilk Haze (fotografiert in White 612)

6	6	6	7	7	x 25g

NADELN

1 Paar Nr. 4.
1 Paar Nr. 3,5

EXTRAS

Maschenmarkierer (Mm)
Hilfsnadeln

MASCHENPROBE

20 M und 26 R = 10 x 10 cm, glatt re gestr mit Ndl Nr. 4 und je
1 einem Fd in Fbe A und B zus gestr.

SPEZIELLE ABKÜRZUNGEN

2übzAbn = 2 M wie zum 2 M re zus-str zus abh, 1 M re,
die 2 abgeh M überziehen.

3übzAbn = 3 M wie zum 3 M re zus-str zus abh, 1 M re,
die 3 abgeh M überziehen.

RÜCKENTEIL

126 (140: 154: 168: 182) M mit Ndl Nr. 3,5 und je einem Fd in
Fbe A und B zus anschl.

R 1 (Hinr): 1 M re, *1 M li, 1 M re, ab * wdhl bis zur letzten M,
1 M re.

R 2: 1 M re, *1 M li, 1 M re, ab * wdhl bis zur letzten M, 1 M re.
Die beiden R bilden das Rippenmuster und werden wdhl bis
4 cm erreicht sind, enden mit einer Rückr.
Wechseln zur Ndl Nr. 4.

Nächste R (Hinr): Re bis zum Ende, dabei gleichmäßig
36 (40: 44: 48: 52) M abn = 90 (100: 110: 120: 130) M.
Mit einer Linksr beg und fortlfd glatt re str bis 35 (36: 37:
38: 39) cm erreicht sind, enden mit einer Rückr.

Armausschnitte

Am Anf der nächsten 2 R je 3 M abk = 84 (94: 104: 114: 124) M.

Nächste R (Hinr): 1 M re, 2übzAbn, re bis zu den letzten
3 M, 2 M re zus-str, 1 M re.

Nächste R: Li.
Die beiden letzten R noch 1 x wdhl = 80 (90: 100: 110: 120) M.
Nach einer Armausschnittlänge von 21 (22: 23: 24: 25) cm
enden mit einer Rückr.

Rückw Halsausschnitt und Schulterschrägen

Nächste R (Hinr): 24 (28: 32: 36: 40) M re, Arbeit wenden,
die restl M auf einer Hilfsndl stilllegen, beide Seiten getrennt
beenden.
Am Halsausschnitt am Anf der nächsten R und am Anf der folg
2. R je 2 M abk, **gleichzeitig** am Anf der 2. R und am Anf der
folg 2. R je 6 (8: 9: 10: 12) M abk.
Nach 1 R die restl 8 (8: 10: 12: 12) M abk.
Die stillgelegten M aufn, mit neuem Fd in einer Hinr die mittl
32 (34: 36: 38: 40) M abk, re str bis zum Ende = 24 (28: 32: 36: 40) M.
Die 2. Seite gegengleich beenden.

LINKES VORDERTEIL

103 (117: 131: 145: 159) M mit Ndl Nr. 3,5 und je einem Fd in Fbe
A und B zus anschl.

R 1 (Hinr): *1 M li, 1 M re, ab * wdhl bis zur letzten M, 1 M re.

R 2: *1 M li, 1 M re, ab * wdhl bis zur letzten M, 1 M re.
Weiter im Rippenmuster str bis 4 cm erreicht sind, enden mit
einer Rückr.
Wechseln zur Ndl Nr. 4.

Nächste R (Hinr): Im Rippenmuster bis zu den letzten 7 M,
dabei gleichmäßig 26 (30: 34: 38.42) M abn, einen Mm auf die re
Ndl, 7 M im Rippenmuster = 77 (87: 97: 107: 117) M.

Nächste R (Rückr): 7 M im Rippenmuster, den Mm
umhängen, li bis zum Ende.

Nächste R: Re bis zum Mm, den Mm umhängen, 7 M im
Rippenmuster.
Die 7 M am vord Rand werden weiter im Rippenmuster gestr,
alle übrigen M glatt re.
Gerade str bis 40 (42: 44: 48: 50) R unterhalb der
Armausschnitte, enden mit einer Rückr.

Vord Halsausschnitt
Größe 1 speziell
Nächste R (Hinr): Re bis 2 M vor dem Mm, 2 M re zus-str, den Mm umhängen, 7 M im Rippenmuster.
3 R str.
Die letzten 4 R noch 2 x wdhl = 74 M.
Größe 2, 3, 4 und 5 speziell
Nächste R (Hinr): Re bis 3 M vor dem Mm, 3 M re zus-str, den Mm umhängen, 7 M im Rippenmuster.
1 R str.
Nächste R (Hinr): Re bis 2 M vor dem Mm, 2 M re zus-str, den Mm umhängen, 7 M im Rippenmuster.
1 R str.
Die letzten 4 R noch – (-: 4: 6: 10) x wdhl = - (84: 82: 86: 84) M.
Alle Größen
Nächste R (Hinr): Re bis 2 M vor dem Mm, 2 M re zus-str, den Mm umhängen, 7 M im Rippenmuster.
1 R str.
Die beiden letzten R noch 13 (18: 11: 9: 2) x wdhl = 60 (65: 70: 76: 81) M.
Armausschnitt
Nächste R (Hinr): 3 M abk, re str bis 2 M vor dem Mm, 2 M re zus-str, den Mm umhängen, 7 M im Rippenmuster = 56 (61: 66: 72: 77) M.
1 R str.
Nächste R (Hinr): 1 M re, **2übzAbn**, re bis 2 M vor dem Mm, 2 M re zus-str, den Mm umhängen, 7 M im Rippenmuster.
1 R str.
Die beiden letzten R noch 1 x wdhl = 52 (57: 62: 68: 73) M.
Das Muster korrekt einhalten, am Halsausschnitt wie angegeben in der nächsten R und 24 (25: 26: 28: 29) x in jeder folg 2. R je 1 M abn = 27 (31: 35: 39: 43) M.
Wenn die gleiche Länge erreicht ist wie beim Rückenteil vor Beg der Schulterschrägen, enden mit einer Rückr.
Schulterschräge
Nächste R (Hinr): 6 (8: 9: 10: 12) M abk, re bis zum Mm, den Mm umhängen, 7 M im Rippenmuster.
Nächste R: 7 M im Rippenmuster, den Mm umhängen, li bis zum Ende.
Die beiden letzten R noch 1 x wdhl = 15 (15: 17: 19: 19) M.
Nächste R: 8 (8: 10: 12: 12) M abk, den Mm umhängen, 7 M im Rippenmuster = 7 M.
Nächste R: 7 M im Rippenmuster.
Die restl 7 M für die Halsblende auf einer Hilfsndl stilllegen.

RECHTES VORDERTEIL
103 (117: 131: 145: 159) M mit Ndl Nr. 3,5 und je einem Fd in Fbe A und B zus anschl.
R 1 (Hinr): *1 M re, 1 M li, ab * wdhl bis zur letzten M, 1 M re.
R 2: 1 M re, *1 M li, 1 M re, ab * wdhl bis zum Ende.
Weiter im Rippenmuster str bis 4 cm erreicht sind, enden mit einer Rückr.
Wechseln zur Ndl Nr. 4.
Nächste R (Hinr): 7 M im Rippenmuster, einen Mm auf die re Ndl, re bis zum Ende, dabei gleichmäßig 26 (30: 34: 38: 42) M abn = 77 (87: 97: 107: 117) M.
Nächste R (Rückr): Li bis zum Mm, den Mm umhängen, 7 M im Rippenmuster.
Nächste R: 7 M im Rippenmuster, den Mm umhängen, re bis zum Ende.
Die 7 M am vord Rand werden weiter im Rippenmuster gestr, alle übrigen M glatt re.

Gerade str bis 40 (42: 44: 48: 50) R unterhalb der Armausschnitte, enden mit einer Rückr.
Vord Halsausschnitt
Größe 1 speziell
Nächste R (Hinr): 7 M im Rippenmuster, den Mm umhängen, 2übzAbn, re bis zum Ende.
3 R str.
Die letzten 4 R noch 2 x wdhl = 74 M.
Größe 2, 3, 4 und 5 speziell
Nächste R (Hinr): 7 M im Rippenmuster, den Mm umhängen, 3übzAbn, re str bis zum Ende.
1 R str.
Nächste R (Hinr): 7 M im Rippenmuster, den Mm umhängen, 3übzAbn, re str bis zum Ende.
1 R str.
Die letzten 4 R noch – (-: 4: 6: 10) x wdhl = - (84: 82: 86: 84) M.
Alle Größen
Nächste R (Hinr): 7 M im Rippenmuster, den Mm umhängen, 2übzAbn, re str bis zum Ende.
1 R str.
Die beiden letzten R noch 13 (18: 11: 9: 2) x wdhl = 60 (65: 70: 76: 81) M.
Armausschnitt
Nächste R (Hinr): 7 M im Rippenmuster, den Mm hängen, 2übzAbn, re str bis zum Ende.
Nächste R (Rückr): 3 M abk, li str bis zum Ende = 56 (61: 66: 72: 77) M.
Nächste R (Hinr): 7 M im Rippenmuster, den Mm umhängen, 2übzAbn, re str bis zu den letzten 3 M, 2 M re zus-str, 1 M re.
1 R str.
Die beiden letzten R noch 1 x wdhl = 52 (57: 62: 68: 73) M.
Das Muster korrekt einhalten, am Halsausschnitt wie angegeben in der nächsten R und 24 (25: 26: 28: 29) x in jeder folg 2. R je 1 M abn = 27 (31: 35: 39: 43) M.
Wenn die gleiche Länge erreicht ist wie beim Rückenteil vor Beg der Schulterschrägen, enden mit einer Hinr.
Schulterschräge
Nächste R (Rückr): 6 (8: 9: 10: 12) M abk, li bis zum Mm, den Mm umhängen, 7 M im Rippenmuster.
Nächste R: 7 M im Rippenmuster, den Mm umhängen, re bis zum Ende.
Die beiden letzten R noch 1 x wdhl = 15 (15: 17: 19: 19) M.
Nächste R: 8 (8: 10: 12: 12) M abk, den Mm umhängen, 7 M im Rippenmuster = 7 M.
Nächste R: 7 M im Rippenmuster.
Die restl 7 M für die Halsblende auf einer Hilfsndl stilllegen.

ÄRMEL
56 (60: 68: 72: 80) M mit Ndl Nr. 3,5 und je einem Fd in Fbe A und B zus anschl.
R 1 (Hinr): 1 M re, *1 M li, 1 M re, ab * wdhl bis zur letzten M, 1 M re.
R 2: 1 M re, *1 M li, 1 M re, ab * wdhl bis zur letzten M, 1 M re.
Weiter im Rippenmuster str bis 9 cm erreicht sind, enden mit einer Rückr.
Wechseln zur Ndl Nr. 4.
Nächste R (Hinr): Re str bis zum Ende, dabei gleichmäßig 10 (10: 8: 8: 6) M zun = 66 (70: 76: 80: 86) M.
Weiter glatt re str, dabei in der 9. (9.: 8.: 8.: 7.) R und in jeder folg 10. (10.: 12.: 12.: 14.) R bds je 1 M zun = 84 (88: 92: 96: 100) M.
Nach einer Länge von 50 (51: 52: 53: 54) M, enden mit einer Rückr. **Armkugel**

Am Anf der nächsten 2 R je 3 M abk = 78 (82: 86: 90: 94) M.

Nächste R (Hinr): I M re, 2übzAbn, re bis zu den letzten 3 M, 2 M re zus-str, I M re.

Nächste R: Li.

Die beiden letzten R noch I x wdhl = 74 (78: 82: 86: 90) M.

4 R glatt re str.

Alle M abk.

FERTIGSTELLUNG

Alle Teile dämpfen, siehe Informationsseite.

Beide Schulternähte schließen.

Halsblende

Von re mit Ndl Nr. 3,5 die 7 M auf der Hilfsndl im re Vorderteil weiter im Rippenmuster str, dabei in einer Rückr beg, bis der Streifen bis zur Mitte der rückw Halsausschnittkante passt, danach alle M im Muster abk.

Die Halsblende für das li Vorderteil genauso str, dabei in einer Hinr beg.

Die beiden Blenden mit den Abkettkanten zusammennähen, danach die Blende an der rückw Halsausschnittkante festnähen.

Gürtel (beide gleich)

Von re mit Ndl Nr. 3,5 und je einem Fd in Fbe A und B ab 2,5 cm unterhalb des Beg der vord Schräge aus der re (oder li) Vorderteilkante 8 M aufn und re str.

R I: 4 x (I M re, I M li).

Weiter im Rippenmuster str bis das Band 96,5 (104: 111,5: 119: 126,5) cm lang ist (oder gewünschte Länge), alle M im Muster abk.

Die Ärmel in die Armausschnitte nähen. Die Seiten- und Ärmelnähte schließen, dabei in der re Seitennaht eine Öffnung für den Gürtel offenlassen.

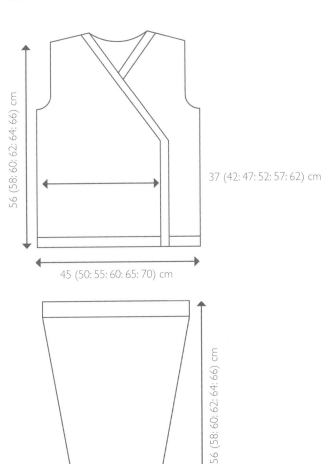

56 (58: 60: 62: 64: 66) cm

37 (42: 47: 52: 57: 62) cm

45 (50: 55: 60: 65: 70) cm

56 (58: 60: 62: 64: 66) cm

HAZEL ••

GRÖSSE
Der Schal ist 46 cm breit und 200 cm lang.

GARN
Rowan Big Wool
7 × 100 g
(fotografiert in Linen 048)

NADELN
1 Paar Nr. 10

MASCHENPROBE
10 M und 12 R = 10 × 10 cm, im Perlmuster gestr mit
Ndl Nr. 10.

SCHAL
46 M mit Ndl Nr. 10 anschl.
R 1 (Hinr): *1 M re, 1 M li, ab * wdhl bis zum Ende.
R 2: *1 M re, 1 M li, ab * wdhl bis zum Ende.
R 3: *1 M li, 1 M re, ab * wdhl bis zum Ende.
R 4: *1 M li, 1 M re, ab * wdhl bis zum Ende.
R 1-4 bilden das doppelte Perlmuster und werden wdhl bis 200
cm erreicht sind, enden mit R 2 des Musters.
Alle M abk.

FERTIGSTELLUNG
Den Schal dämpfen, siehe Informationsseite.

VALENTINA ●●●

GRÖSSEN

Passend für Oberweite

81-86	91-97	102-107	112-117	122-127	cm

Gestrickte Oberweite

90	100	110	120	130	cm

GARN

Rowan Big Wool (fotografiert in White Hot 001)

8	9	10	11	12	× 100 g

NADELN

1 Rundstrickndl Nr. 8, 80 cm lang.
1 Nadelspiel Nr. 8
1 Rundstrickndl Nr. 10, 80 cm lang.
1 Nadelspiel Nr. 10

EXTRAS

Maschenmarkierer (Mm)
Hilfsnadeln

MASCHENPROBE

10 M und 16 Runden = 10 × 10 cm, glatt re gestr mit Ndl Nr. 10; und 12 M und 16 R = 10 × 10 cm, im Perlmuster gestr mit Ndl Nr. 10.

SPEZIELLE ABKÜRZUNG

Mmabh = Den Mm auf die re Ndl heben.

MUSTER

Perlmuster (gestr in Runden)
Rde 1: 1 M re, *1 M li, 1 M re, ab * wdhl bis zum Ende.
Rde 2: 1 M li, *1 M re, 1 M li, ab * wdhl bis zum Ende.
Die beiden Runden werden fortlfd wdhl.
Perlmuster (in Hin- und Rückr gestr)
R 1: 1 M re, *1 M li, 1 M re, ab * wdhl bis zum Ende.
Diese R wird fortlfd wdhl.
Gefächertes Lochmuster (gestr in Runden)
Rde 1: 19 M re.
Rde 2: 1 U, 3 M re zus-str, 13 M re, 3 M re zus-str, 1 U = 17 M.
Rde 3: 17 M re.
Rde 4: 1 U, 3 M re zus-str, 11 M re, 3 M re zus-str, 1 U = 15 M.
Rde 5: 15 M re.
Rde 6: 1 U, 3 M re zus-str, 9 M re, 3 M re zus-str, 1 U = 13 M.
Rde 7: 13 M re.
Rde 8: 1 U, 3 M re zus-str, 7 x (1 U, 7 M re), 1 U, 3 M re zus-str, 1 U = 19 M.
Rde 1-8 werden fortfd wdhl.

Gefächertes Lochmuster (in Hin- und Rückr gestr)
R 1 (Rückr): 19 M li.
R 2: 1 U, 3 M re zus-str, 13 M re, 3 M re zus-str, 1 U = 17 M.
R 3: 17 M li.
R 4: 1 U, 3 M re zus-str, 11 M re, 3 M re zus-str, 1 U = 15 M.
R 5: 15 M li.
R 6: 1 U, 3 M re zus-str, 9 M re, 3 M re zus-str, 1 U = 13 M.
R 7: 13 M li.
R 8: 1 U, 3 M re zus-str, 7 x (1 U, 1 M re), 1 U, 3 M re zus-str, 1 U = 19 M.
R 1-8 bilden das Muster und werden fortlfd wdhl.

HINWEIS

Musterbedingt variiierte die Maschenzahl innerhalb eines Rapportes vom Lochmuster.

BODY

162 (180: 198: 216: 234) M mit der Rundstrickndl Nr. 8 anschl.
In Runden str wie folgt, dabei beachten, dass in der 1. Rde die M nicht verdreht sind, Anf und Ende jeder Rde mark:
Rippenmuster Rde: *1 M re, 1 M li, ab * wdhl bis zum Ende.
Diese Rde wdhl bis 5 cm erreicht sind.
Wechseln zur Rundstsrickndl Nr. 10.
Nächste Rde: Re str bis zum Ende, dabei gleichmäßig 72 (78: 88: 94: 104) M abn = 90 (102: 110: 122: 130) M.
Im Muster str wie folgt:
Basis-Rde: 12 (15: 17: 20: 22) M re, einen Mm auf die re Ndl

M re, 2 x (1 M li, 1 M re), einen Mm auf die re Ndl, 9 x (1 U, 1 M re), 1 U, einen Mm auf die re Ndl, 1 M re, 2 x (1 M li, 1 M re), einen Mm auf die re Ndl, re bis zum Ende = 100 (112: 120: 132: 140) M.

Nächste Rde: Re bis zum Mm, Mmabh, 1 M li, 2 x (1 M re, 1 M li), Mmabh, die nächsten 19 M nach R 1 des Lochmusters str, Mmabh, 1 M li, 2 x (1 M re, 1 M li), Mmabh, re bis zum Ende.
Diese R teilt die M ein für das Lochmuster mit M im Perlmuster an beiden Seiten.
Das Muster korrekt einhalten bis 34 (35: 36: 37: 38) cm, enden mit einer geraden Reihenzahl des Lochmusters.

Armausschnitte
R 1 (Hinr): Re bis zum Mm, Mmabh, im Perlmuster bis zum nächsten Mm, Mmabh, die nächste R des Lochmusters str, Mmabh, im Perlmuster bis zum Mm, Mmabh, 12 (15: 17: 20: 22) M re, Arb wenden
Die restl 45 (51: 55: 61: 65) M für das Rückenteil auf einer Hilfsndl stilllegen.

VORDERTEIL
Das Muster in Hin- und Rückr str wie angegeben, nach ca. 14 (14: 15: 15: 16) cm ab den Armausschnitten enden nach R 1 des Lochmusters = 53 (59: 63: 69: 73) M.

Vord Halsausschnitt
Nächste R (Hinr): 17 (20: 22: 25: 27) M im Muster, Arbeit wenden, die restl M auf einer Hilfsndl stilllegen, beide Seiten getrennt beenden.
Am Halsausschnitt in den nächsten 3 (4: 4: 4: 4) R je 1 M abn = 14 (16: 18: 21: 23) M.
3 (2: 2: 2: 2) R str.
Alle M abk.
Die stillgelegten M aufn, die mittl 19 M auf einer Hilfsndl stilllegen, mit neuem Fd in einer Hinr im Muster str bis zum Ende = 17 (20: 22: 25: 27) M.
Die 2. Seite gegengleich beenden.

RÜCKENTEIL
Zurück zu den stillgelegten 45 (51: 55: 61: 65) M auf der Hilfsndl
für das Rückenteil, glatt re str bis dieselbe Länge erreicht ist wie beim Vorderteil vor Beg des Halsausschnittes, enden mit einer Rückr.
Noch 2 R glatt re str.
Rückw Halsausschnitt und Schulterschrägen
Nächste R (Hinr): 16 (19: 21: 24: 26) M re, Arbeit wenden, die restl M auf einer Hilfsndl stilllegen, beide Seiten getrennt beenden.
Am Halsausschnitt in den nächsten 2 (3: 3: 3: 3) R je 1 M abn = 14 (16: 18: 21: 23) M.
2 (1: 1: 1: 1) R gerade str.
Alle M abk.
Die stillgelegten M aufn, mit neuem Fd in einer Hinr die mittl 13 M abk, re str bis zum Ende = 16 (19: 21: 24: 26) M.
Die 2. Seite gegengleich beenden.

ÄRMEL
Beide Schulternähte schließen.
Mit dem Nadelspiel Nr. 10 in der Mitte des unteren Armausschnittes beg und aus der Armausschnittkante bis zur Schulternaht 20 (21: 21: 21: 22) M aufn und re str, danach von der Schulternaht bis zur unteren Mitte 20 (21: 21: 21: 22) M = 40 (42: 42: 42: 44) M.

Im Muster str wie folgt:
Rde 1: *1 M li, 1 M re, ab * wdhl bis zum Ende.
Rde 2: *1 M re, 1 M li, ab * wdhl bis zum Ende.
Die 2 Runden bilden das Perlmuster und werden wdhl bis 34 (35: 35: 36,5: 36,5) cm erreicht sind.
Nächste Rde: *2 M re zus-str, ab * wdhl bis zum Ende = 20 (21: 21: 21: 22) M.
Wechseln zum Nadelspiel Nr. 8.
5 cm im Rippenmuster str so wie beim Body angegeben, danach alle M locker im Muster abk.

FERTIGSTELLUNG
Den Pullover dämpfen, siehe Informationsseite.
Rollkragen
Von re mit dem Nadelspiel Nr. 8 aus der li vord Halsausschnittkante 9 M auf und re str, die 19 M auf der Hilfsndl im Vorderteil re str, aus der re vord Halsausschnittkante 9 M aufn und re str, aus der re rückw Halsausschnittkante 4 M aufn und re str, aus der rückw Halsausschnittkante 13 M aufn und re str und aus der li rückw Halsausschnittkante 4 M aufn und re str = 58 M.
10 cm im 1x1 Rippenmuster in Runden str, danach wechseln zum Nadelspiel Nr. 10.
Nach weiteren 10 cm im Rippenmuster alle M im Muster locker abk.

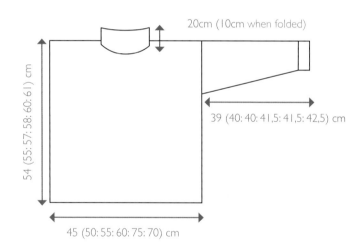

20cm (10cm when folded)

54 (55: 57: 58: 60: 61) cm

39 (40: 40: 41,5: 41,5: 42,5) cm

45 (50: 55: 60: 75: 70) cm

MIDWAY ●●

GRÖSSEN
Passend für Oberweite

81-86	91-97	102-107	112-117	122-127	cm

Gestrickte Oberweite

101,5	111,5	121,5	134	143,5	cm

GARN
Rowan Kid Classic
A Pumice 888

4	4	5	5	5	× 50g

B Feather 828

1	1	1	1	1	× 50g

C Cement 890

1	1	1	1	1	× 50g

NADELN
1 Paar Nr. 4
1 Paar Nr. 5,5
Je 1 Rundstrickndl Nr. 4 und 5,5, höchstens 60 cm lang (nur für die Ärmel)

EXTRAS
Fremdgarn oder Hilfsnadeln
5 Knöpfe

MASCHENPROBE
16 M und 24 R = 10 x 10 cm, glatt re gestr mit Ndl Nr. 5,5.

BODY
230 (254: 278: 310: 334) M mit Ndl Nr. 4 anschl.
R 1 (Hinr): 1 M re, *2 M li, 2 M re, ab * wdhl bis zur letzten M, 1 M re.
R 2: 1 M re, *2 M li, 2 M re, ab * wdhl bis zur letzten M, 1 M re.
Die beiden R bilden das Rippenmuster und werden wdhl bis 5 cm erreicht sind, enden mit einer Rückr.
Wechseln zur Ndl Nr. 5,5.
Nächste R (Hinr): Re bis zum Ende, dabei gleichmäßig 75 (83: 91: 103: 112) M abn = 155 (171: 187: 207: 222) M.
Mit einer Linksr beg und fortlfd glatt re str bis 26 (27: 28: 29: 30) cm erreicht sind, enden mit einer Rückr.
Armausschnitte
Nächste R (Hinr): 37 (41: 45: 50: 54) M re, diese M für das re Vorderteil auf einer Hilfsndl stilllegen, die nächsten 81 (89: 97: 107: 114) M für das Rückenteil re str, Arb wenden, die restl 37 (41: 45: 50: 54) M für das li Vorderteil auf einer 2. Hilfsndl stilllegen.

RÜCKENTEIL
Weiter glatt re bis 18 (18: 19: 19: 20) cm ab Beg der Armausschnitte erreicht sind, enden mit einer Rückr.

Rückw Halsausschnitt und Schulterschrägen
R 1 (Hinr): 27 (31: 35: 40: 43) M re, Arbeit wenden, die restl M auf einer Hilfsndl stilllegen, beide Seiten getrennt beenden.
R 2: 3 M abk, li str bis zum Ende.
R 3: 6 (7: 8: 10: 11) M abk, re bis zum Ende.
R 4-5: Wie R 2-3 = 9 (11: 13: 14: 15) M.
R 6: 3 (3: 3: 3: 4) M abk, li bis zum Ende = 6 (8: 10: 11: 11) M. Alle M abk.
Die stillgelegten M aufn, mit neuem Fd in einer Hinr die mittl 27 (27: 27: 27: 28) M abk, re str bis zum Ende = 27 (31: 35: 40: 43) M.
Die 2. Seite gegengleich beenden.

LINKES VORDERTEIL
Die M auf der 2. Hilfsndl aufn, mit Fbe A in einer Hinr beg und die 37 (41: 45: 50: 54) M re str bis zum Ende der R.
Glatt re str bis 9 (9: 10: 10: 11) cm ab den Armausschnitten erreicht sind, enden mit einer Hinr.
Vord Halsausschnitt
Nächste R (Rückr): 6 (6: 6: 6: 7) M abk, li bis zum Ende.
1 R str.
Nächste R: 5 (5: 5: 5: 6) M abk, li bis zum Ende.
1 R str.
Nächste R: 4 M abk, li str bis zum Ende.
Am Halsausschnitt in den nächsten 3 R je 1 M abn, danach 1 x in der folg 2. R 1 M abn = 18 (22: 26: 31: 33) M.

Gerade str bis das Vorderteil die gleiche Länge erreicht hat wie das Rückenteil vor Beg der Schulterschrägen, enden mit einer Rückr.

Schulterschräge
Am Anf der nächsten R und am Anf der folg 2. R je 6 (7: 8: 10: 11) M abk.
Nach 1 R die restl 6 (8: 10: 11: 11) M abk.

RECHTES VORDERTEIL
Die M auf der 1. Hilfsndl aufn, mit Fbe A in einer Rückr beg und die 37 (41: 45: 50: 54) M li str bis zum Ende der R.
Glatt re str bis 9 (9: 10: 10: 11) cm ab den Armausschnitten erreicht sind, enden mit einer Rückr.
Das re Vorderteil gegengleich zum li Vorderteil beenden.

ÄRMEL
Das Teil dämpfen, siehe Informationsseite.
Beide Schulternähte schließen.
Mit der Rundstrickndl Nr. 5,5 und Fbe A in der unteren Mitte des Armausschnittes beg und aus vord Armausschnittkante bis zur Schulternaht 32 (32: 32: 36: 36) M aufn und re str, danach von der Schulternaht bis zur unteren Mitte 32 (32: 32: 36: 36) M aufn und re str, einen Markierungsring auf die re Ndl hängen = 64 (64: 64: 72: 72) M.
In Runden 10 cm glatt re str.
Wechseln zur Fbe B und weitere 3 cm glatt re str, danach mit Fbe C weiter glatt re str bis 28 (29: 29: 30,5: 30,5) cm erreicht sind.
Nächste Rde: *6 (6: 6: 7: 7) M re, 2 M re zus-str, ab * wdhl bis zum Ende = 56 (56: 56: 64: 64) M.
Nächste Rde: Re.
Nächste Rde: *5 (5: 5: 6: 6) M re, 2 M re zus-str, ab * wdhl bis zum Ende = 48 (48: 48: 56: 56) M.
Nächste Rde: Re.
Nächste Rde: Re str bis zum Ende, dabei gleichmäßig 4 (0: 0: 4: 4) M abn = 44 (48: 48: 52: 52) M.

Bündchen
Wechseln zur Rundstrickndl Nr. 4
Nächste Rde: *2 M re, 2 M li, ab * wdhl bis zum Ende.
Weiter im Rippenmuster str bis 8 cm erreicht sind, danach alle M locker im Muster abk.

FERTIGSTELLUNG
Knopfblende
Von re mit Ndl Nr. 5,5 und Fbe A aus der li Vorderteilkante von der Halsausschnittkante bis zur Anschlagkante 82 (86: 90: 94: 98) M aufn und re str.
R 1 (Rückr): 2 M li, *2 M re, 2 M li, ab * wdhl bis zum Ende.
R 2: 2 M re, *2 M li, 2 M re, ab * wdhl bis zum Ende.
Weiter im Rippenmuster str bis 5 cm erreicht sind, danach alle M im Muster abk.
Auf der Blende 4 Knöpfe markieren: Den untersten 2,5 cm oberhalb der Anschlagkante, der oberste kommt 2,5 cm oberhalb der Halsausschnittkante in die Halsblende, die restl 3 Knöpfe gleichmäßig dazwischen verteilen.
Knopflochblende
Von re mit Ndl Nr. 5,5 und Fbe A aus der re Vorderteilkante von der Anschlagkante bis zur Halsausschnittkante 82 (86: 90: 94: 98) M aufn und re str.
R 1 (Rückr): 2 M li, *2 M re, 2 M li, ab * wdhl bis zum Ende.
R 2: 2 M re, *2 M li, 2 M re, ab * wdhl bis zum Ende.
Nach 2,5 cm im Rippenmuster enden mit einer Rückr.

Knopflochr (Hinr): 4 x (im Muster bis zum markierten Knopfloch, 2 M im Muster zus-str, 1 U), im Muster str bis zum Ende.
Nach 5 cm im Rippenmuster alle M im Muster abk.
Halsblende
Von re mit Ndl Nr. 5,5 und Fbe A aus dem oberen Rand der Knopflochblende 12 M aufn und re str, aus der re vord Halsausschnittkante 37 (37: 37: 37: 41) M aufn und re str, aus der re rückw Halsausschnittkante 14 (14: 14: 14: 15) M aufn und re str, aus der rückw Halsausschnittkante 40 (40: 40: 40: 42) M aufn und re str, aus der li rückw Halsausschnittkante 14 (14: 14 14: 15) M aufn und re str, aus der li vord Halsausschnittkante 37 (37: 37: 37: 41) M aufn und re str und aus dem oberen Rand der Knopfblende 12 M aufn und re str = 166 (166: 166: 166: 178) M.
R 1 (Rückr): 2 M li, *2 M re, 2 M li, ab * wdhl bis zum Ende.
R 2: 2 M re, *2 M li, 2 M re, ab * wdhl bis zum Ende.
Weiter im Rippenmuster str bis 2,5 cm erreicht sind, enden mit einer Rückr.
Knopflochr (Hinr): 6 M im Muster, 2 M zus-str, 1 U, im Muster bis zum Ende.
Nach 5 cm im Rippenmuster alle M im Muster abk. Die Knöpfe annähen.

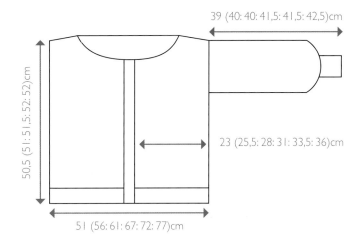

39 (40: 40: 41,5: 41,5: 42,5)cm

50,5 (51: 51,5: 52: 52)cm

23 (25,5: 28: 31: 33,5: 36)cm

51 (56: 61: 67: 72: 77)cm

PEARL ●●

GRÖSSEN

Passend für Oberweite

81-86	91-97	102-107	112-117	122-127	cm

Gestrickte Oberweite

99	114	119	129	144	cm

GARN

Rowan Alpaca Classic (fotografiert in Feather Grey Melange 101)

13	14	14	15	16	× 25 g

NADELN

1 Paar Nr. 4.
1 Paar Nr. 5

EXTRAS

4 Maschenmarkierer
2 Hilfsnadeln

MASCHENPROBE

16 M und 22 R = 10 x 10 cm, im Muster und glatt re gestr mit Ndl Nr. 5 und doppeltem Fd.

HINWEIS

Wenn beim vord Halsausschnitt und an den Schultern nicht mehr ein vollständiger Rapport mit 12 M gestr werden kann, werden die restl M glatt re str.

RÜCKENTEIL

108 (120: 132: 144: 156) M mit Ndl Nr. 4 und doppeltem Fd anschl.

R 1 (Hinr): 1 M abh, *2 M li, 2 M re, ab * wdhl bis zu den letzten 3 M, 2 M li, 1 M re.

R 2: 1 M abh, 2 M re, *2 M li, 2 M re, ab * wdhl bis zur letzten M, 1 M re.

Die beiden R bilden das Rippenmuster und werden wdhl bis 10 cm erreicht sind, enden mit einer Rückr.

Wechseln zur Ndl Nr. 5.

Nächste R (Hinr): Re str bis zum Ende, dabei gleichmäßig 27 (27: 35: 39: 39) M abn = 81 (93: 97: 105: 117) M.

Nächste R: Li. **

Mit einer Rechtsr beg und fortlfd glatt re str bis 32 (33: 34: 35: 36) cm erreicht sind, enden mit einer Rückr.

Anf und Ende der letzten R für das Ende der seitl Schlitze markieren.

Weiter glatt re str bis 20 (21: 22: 23: 24) cm ab der mark R erreicht sind, enden mit einer Rückr.

Rückw Halsausschnitt und Schulterschrägen

R 1 (Hinr): 27 (33: 34: 38: 43) M re, Arbeit wenden, die restl M auf einer Hilfsndl stilllegen, beide Seiten getrennt beenden = 27 (33: 34: 38: 43) M.

Am Halsausschnitt am Anf der nächsten R 4 (5: 5: 5: 5) M abk, für die Schulterschräge am Anf der 2. R und am Anf der folg 2. R je 8 (10: 10: 11: 13) M abk.

Nach 1 R die restl 7 (8: 9: 11: 12) M abk.

Alle M abk.

Die stillgelegten M aufn, mit neuem Fd in einer Hinr die mittl 27 (27: 29: 29: 31) M abk, re str bis zum Ende = 27 (33: 34: 38: 43) M.

Die 2. Seite gegengleich beenden.

VORDERTEIL

Das Vorderteil str wie das Rückenteil, angegeben bis **.

Im Muster str wie folgt:

R 1 (Hinr): 1 (1: 3: 1: 1) M re, *2 M re, 2 M re zus-str, 1 U, 8 M re, ab * wdhl bis zu den letzten 8 (8: 10: 8: 8) M, 2 M re, 2 M re zus-str, 1 U, 3 (3: 5: 3: 3) M re.

R 2 und jede folg Rückr: Li.

R 3: 1 (1: 3: 1: 1) M re, *1 M re, 2 x (2 M re zus-str, 1 U), 7 M re, ab * wdhl bis zu den letzten 8 (8: 10: 8: 8) M, 1 M re, 2 x (2 M re zus-str, 1 U), re bis zum Ende =

R 5: Wie R 1.

R 7: Re.

R 9: 1 (1: 3: 1: 1) M re, *8 M re, 2 M re zus-str, 1 U, 2 M re, ab * wdhl bis zu den letzten 8 (8: 10: 8: 8) M, re bis zum Ende.

R 11: 1 (1: 3: 1: 1) M re, *7 M re, 2 x (2 M re zus-str, 1 U), 1 M re, ab * wdhl bis zu den letzten 8 (8: 10: 8: 8) M, re bis zum Ende.

R 13: Wie R 9.

R 15: Re.

R 16: Li.

Diese 16 R bilden das Muster und werden wdhl bis 32 (33: 34: 35: 36) cm erreicht sind, enden mit einer Rückr.

Anf und Ende der letzten R für das Ende der seitl Schlitze markieren. **

Das Muster korrekt einhalten bis 14 (15: 16: 17: 18) cm ab der mark R erreicht sind, enden mit einer Rückr.

Vord Halsausschnitt

Nächste R (Hinr): 32 (37: 39: 43: 48) M im Muster, Arbeit wenden, die restl M auf einer Hilfsndl stilllegen, beide Seiten getrennt beenden.

Am Halsausschnitt in der nächsten R und in den folg 5 (5: 7: 7: 7) R je 1 M abn, danach 3 (3: 2: 2: 2) x in jeder folg 2. R je 1 M abn = 23 (28: 29: 33: 38) M.

Gerade str bis die gleiche Länge erreicht ist wie beim Rückenteil vor Beg der Schulterschrägen, enden mit einer Rückr.

Schulterschräge

Am Anf der nächsten R und am Anf der folg 2. R je 8 (10: 10: 11: 13) M abk.

Nach 1 R die restl 7 (8: 9: 11: 12) M abk.

Die stillgelegten M aufn, mit neuem Fd in einer Hinr die mittl 17 (19: 19: 19: 21) M abk, im Muster str bis zum Ende = 32 (37: 39: 43: 48) M.

Die 2. Seite gegengleich beenden.

ÄRMEL

46 (50: 50: 54: 54) M mit Ndl Nr. 4 und doppeltem Fd anschl.

R 1: 1 M re, *2 M li, 2 M re, ab * wdhl bis zur letzten M, 1 M re.

Weiter im Rippenmuster str bis 8 cm erreicht sind, enden mit einer Rückr.

Wechseln zur Ndl Nr. 5.

Nächste R (Hinr): Re str bis zum Ende, dabei gleichmäßig 10 (10: 10: 12: 12) M abn = 36 (40: 40: 42: 42) M.

Mit einer Linksr beg und 9 R glatt re str, enden mit einer Rückr.

In der nächsten R und in jeder folg 4. R bds je 1 M zun bis 64 (68: 70: 74: 76) M erreicht sind.

Nach einer Länge von 43 (44: 45: 46: 47) cm enden mit einer Rückr.

Alle M abk.

FERTIGSTELLUNG

Alle Teile dämpfen, siehe Informationsseite.

Die re Schulternaht schließen.

Kragen

Von re mit Ndl Nr. 4 und doppeltem Fd aus der ganzen Halsausschnittkante 118 (126: 130: 134: 146) M aufn und re str, dabei an der li Vorderteilkante beg und am Ende der rückw li Halsausschnittkante enden.

R 1: 1 M re, 2 M re, 2 M li, ab * wdhl bis zur letzten M, 1 M re.

Weiter im Rippenmuster str bis 8 cm erreicht sind, enden mit einer Rückr. Alle M **locker** im Muster abk.

Die li Schulternaht und die seitl Kragennaht schließen. Die Ärmel mit der Mitte der Abkettkante auf die Schulternähte heften und an den seitl Rändern zwischen den mark R festnähen. Die Seitennähte bis zu den mark R schließen. Die Ärmelnähte schließen.

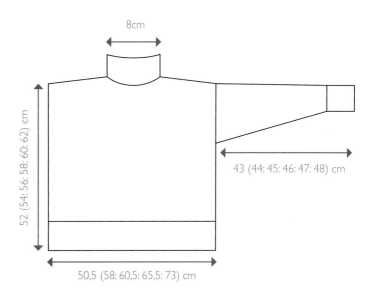

8cm

52 (54: 56: 58: 60: 62) cm

43 (44: 45: 46: 47: 48) cm

50,5 (58: 60,5: 65,5: 73) cm

HERRINGBONE ●●●

GRÖSSEN

Passend für Oberweite

| 81-86 | 91-97 | 102-107 | 112-117 | 122-127 | cm |

Gestrickte Oberweite

| 90 | 103 | 113 | 123 | 133 | cm |

GARN

Rowan Kid Classic (fotografiert in Floss 899)

| 8 | 8 | 9 | 9 | 10 | × 50g |

NADELN

1 Paar Nr. 5,5

1 Rundstrickndl Nr. 5,5, 80 cm lang.

EXTRAS

Hilfsnadeln

3 Maschenmarkierer (Mm)

MASCHENPROBE

18 M und 23 R = 10 x 10 cm, glatt re gestr mit Ndl Nr. 5,5.
28 M und 24 R = 10 x 10 cm, im Fischgrätmuster gestr mit Ndl Nr. 5,5.

Fischgrätmuster

R 1 (Hinr): *1 M abh, ohne die M von der li Ndl fallen zu lassen, die 2. M auf der li Ndl re verschr str, danach die 1. M re verschr str, beide M zus- von der li Ndl fallen lassen, ab * wdhl bis zum Ende.
R 2: 1 M abh, *die 2. M auf der li Ndl li str, danach die 1. M li str, beide M zus von der li Ndl fallen lassen.
Die beiden R bilden das Muster und werden fortlfd wdhl.

RÜCKENTEIL

109 (123: 135: 147: 159) M mit Ndl Nr. 5,5 anschl.
R 1 (Hinr): 1 M abh, *1 M li, 1 M re verschr, ab * wdhl bis zu den letzten 2 M, 1 M li, 1 M re.
R 2: 1 M abh, 1 M re, *1 M li verschr, 1 M re, ab * wdhl bis zur letzten M, 1 M re.
Die beiden R bilden das Rippenmuster und werden wdhl bis 7 cm erreicht sind, enden mit einer Hinr.
Nächste R (Rückr): Li bis zum Ende der R, dabei gleichmäßig 18 (22: 24: 26: 28) M zun = 127 (145: 159: 173: 187) M. **
Mit R 1 des Fischgrätmusters beg, die 2 R fortlfd wdhl bis 37 (38: 38: 39: 39) cm erreicht sind, enden mit einer Rückr.
Anf und Ende der letzten R für den Beg der Armausschnitte mit einem Fd markieren.
Nach weiteren 48 (48: 50: 50: 52) R enden mit einer Rückr.

Rückw Halsausschnitt und Schulterschrägen

R 1 (Hinr): 45 (53: 59: 66: 72) M im Muster, Arbeit wenden, die restl M auf einer Hilfsndl stilllegen, beide Seiten getrennt beenden.
Am Halsausschnitt am Anf der nächsten R 3 (3: 3: 4: 4) M abk, danach am Anf jeder folg 2. R 1 x 3 M und 2 x je 2 M abk, **gleichzeitig** für die Schulterschräge am Anf der 2. R und der folg 2. R je 8 (10: 12: 13: 15) M abk, danach 1 x 9 (11: 12: 14: 15) M.
Nach 1 R die restl 10 (12: 13: 14: 16) M abk.
Die stillgelegten M aufn, mit neuem Fd in einer Hinr die mittl 37 (39: 41: 41: 43) M abk, im Muster str bis zum Ende = 45 (53: 59: 66: 72) M.
Die 2. Seite gegengleich beenden.

VORDERTEIL

Genauso str wie beim Rückenteil bis 16 (16: 14: 14: 12) R unterhalb von **, enden mit einer Rückr.

V-Ausschnitt

Nächste R (Hinr): 63 (72: 79: 86: 93) M im Muster, Arbeit wenden, die restl M auf einer Hilfsndl stilllegen, beide Seiten getrennt beenden.
*** Das Muster korrekt einhalten, am Halsausschnitt in der nächsten R und in den folg - (-: -: 2: -) R je 1 M abn, danach 3 (4: 4: 3: 5) x in jeder folg 4. (3.: 3.: 3.: 2.) R je 1 M abn = 59 (67: 74: 80: 87) M.
Weitere 2 (2: -: 1: -) R im Muster str = 16 (16: 14: 14: 12) R insgesamt für Halsausschnitt, enden mit einer Rückr.
Den seitl Rand für den Beg des Armausschnittes markieren.
Weitere 48 (48: 50: 50: 52) R str, dabei am Halsausschnitt in der nächsten R und 23 (23: 24: 24: 25) x in jeder folg 2. R je 1 M abn = 35 (43: 49: 55: 61) M.

Das Vorderteil müsste genauso lang sein wie das Rückenteil vor Beg der Schulterschrägen, enden mit einer Rückr.

Schulterschräge

2 R str.

Am Anf der nächsten R und am Anf der folg 2. R je 8 (10: 12: 13: 15) M abk, danach am Anf jeder folg 2. R 1 x 9 (11: 12: 14: 15) M abk und 1 x 10 (12: 13: 15: 16) M abk.

Die stillgelegten M aufn, die mittl M auf einer Sicherheitsndl stilllegen, mit neuem Fd in einer Hinr im Muster str bis zum Ende = 63 (72: 79: 86: 93) M.

Die 2. Seite gegengleich beenden.

ÄRMEL

48 (52: 58: 62: 68) M mit Ndl Nr. 5,5 anschl.

R 1 (Hinr): 1 M re, *1 M li, 1 M re verschr, ab * wdhl bis zur letzten M, 1 M re.

R 2: 1 M re, *1 M li verschr, 1 M re, ab * wdhl bis zur letzten M, 1 M re.

Die beiden letzten R wdhl bis 12 cm erreicht sind, enden mit einer Rückr.

Nächste R (Hinr): Re bis zum Ende der R, dabei gleichmäßig 12 (12: 14: 16: 18) M abn = 36 (40: 44: 46: 50) M.

Mit einer Linksr beg, 13 R glatt re str, enden mit einer Rückr. In der nächsten R und 12 (6: 5: 2: 1) x in jeder folg 2. R bds je 1 M zun, danach in jeder folg 4. (4.: 4.: 4.: 4.) R bds je 1 M zun, bis 82 (82: 86: 86: 90) M erreicht sind.

Nach einer Länge von 51 (52: 53: 54: 55) cm enden mit einer Rückr. Alle M abk.

FERTIGSTELLUNG

Alle Teile dämpfen, siehe Informationsseite.

Beide Schulternähte schließen.

Halsblende

Von re mit der Rundstrickndl Nr. 5,5 an der li Schulternaht beg und die M wie folgt aufn und re str: Aus der li vord Halsausschnittkante bis zur vord Mitte 55 (55: 55: 57: 57) M, einen Mm auf die re Ndl hängen, die M auf der Sicherheitsndl re str und mit einem Fd markieren, aus der re vord Halsausschnittkante 55 (55: 55: 57: 57) M und aus der rückw Halsausschnittkante 37 (39: 41: 41: 43) M, einen Mm auf die re Ndl hängen, in Runden str wie folgt = 148 (150: 152: 156: 158) M.

Rde 1: 1 M li, (1 M re verschr, 1 M li) wdhl bis zum Mm, den Mm umhängen, 1 M re verschr, (1 M li, 1 M re verschr) wdhl bis zum Ende.

Rde 2: Im Muster bis 1 M vor dem Mm, den Mm auf die re Ndl hängen, 2 M wie zum 2 M re zus-str abheben, dabei den 1. Mm entfernen, die 2 abgehobenen M überziehen, im Rippenmuster bis zum Ende.

Rde 3: Im Muster bis 2 M vor dem Mm, 1 M re verschr, einen Mm auf die re Ndl, 2 M wie zum 2 M re zus-str abheben, dabei den 1. Mm entfernen, die 2 abgehobenen M überziehen, im Rippenmuster bis zum Ende.

Rde 4 und 5: Wie Rde 2 und 3.

Rde 6: Wie Rde 2.

Alle M locker im Muster abk, dabei die Abn in der vord Mitte noch 1 x wdhl.

Die Ärmel mit der Mitte der Abkettkante auf die Schulternähte heften, danach die Ärmel an den seitl Rändern zwischen den mark R festnähen. Die Ärmelnähte schließen, dabei die Bündchen ab der Hälfte von der Gegenseite zunähen, weil sie Bündchen nach außen umschlagen werden. Die Seitennähte schließen.

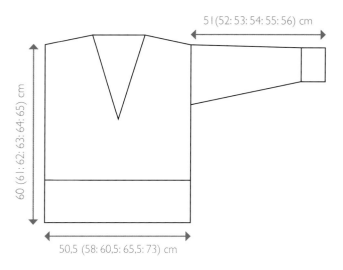

51 (52: 53: 54: 55: 56) cm

60 (61: 62: 63: 64: 65) cm

50,5 (58: 60,5: 65,5: 73) cm

RUMPLED ●●

GRÖSSEN

Passend für Oberweite

81-86	91-97	102-107	112-117	122-127	cm

Gestrickte Oberweite

100	110	120	130	140	cm

GARN

Rowan Brushed Fleece (fotografiert in Cove 251)

7	8	9	10	11	x 50g

NADELN

Je 1 Rundstrickndl Nr. 5, 40 und 80 cm lang.
1 Nadelspiel Nr. 5
1 Rundstrickndl Nr. 6, 40 cm lang.
Je 1 Rundstrickndl Nr. 7, 80 cm lang.
1 Nadelspiel Nr. 7

EXTRAS

8 Maschenmarkierer (Mm)
Hilfsnadeln

MASCHENPROBE

12 M und 17 Runden = 10 x 10 cm, glatt re gestr mit Ndl Nr. 7.

SPEZIELLE ABKÜRZUNGEN

LiZun = Mit der li Ndl den Querfaden zwischen beiden Nadeln von vorne nach hinten aufnehmen und re str, dabei von hinten in die Schlinge einstechen.

ReZun = Mit der li Ndl den Querfaden zwischen beiden Nadeln von hinten nach vorne aufnehmen und re str, dabei von vorne in die Schlinge einstechen.

1 M verdopp = In der nächsten M 1 M zun, dabei 1 x von vorne und 1 x von hinten in die nächste M einstechen und je 1 M re heraus str = 1 Zun.

Mmabh = Den Mm auf die re Ndl heben.

HINWEISE

Der Pullover wird in einem Stück von oben nach unten gestr. Der Halsausschnitt beginnt in Reihen, sobald die M für das Vorderteil angeschlagen wurden, wird in Runden weiter gestr. Die Ärmel werden mit dem Nadelspiel von oben nach unten in Runden gestr.

PASSE

44 (46: 46: 50: 50) M mit der langen Rundstrickndl Nr. 7 anschl, in Hin- und Rückr str wie folgt:

R 1 (Hinr): 1 M re, einen Mm auf die re Ndl, 2 M re, einen Mm auf die re Ndl, 2 (2: 2: 3: 3) M re, einen Mm auf die re Ndl, 2 M re, einen Mm auf die re Ndl, 30 (32: 32: 34: 34) M re, einen Mm auf die re Ndl, 2 M re, einen Mm auf die re Ndl, 2 (2: 2: 3: 3) M re,

einen Mm auf die re Ndl, 2 M re, einen Mm auf die re Ndl, 1 M re = 8 Mm.

R 2 und jede folg Rückr: Li.

R 3: 1 M verdopp, LiZun, Mmabh, 2 M re, Mmabh, ReZun, re bis zum nächsten Mm, LiZun, Mmabh, 2 M re, Mmabh, ReZun, re bis zum nächsten Mm, LiZun, den Mmabh, 2 M re, den Mmabh, ReZun, re bis zum nächsten Mm, LiZun, den Mmabh, 2 M re, den Mmabh, ReZun, 1 M verdopp = 10 Zun, 54 (56: 56: 60: 60) M.

R 5: 1 M verdopp, re bis zum nächsten Mm, LiZun, Mmabh, 2 M re, Mmabh, ReZun, re bis zum nächsten Mm, LiZun, Mmabh, 2 M re, Mmabh, ReZun, re bis zum nächsten Mm, LiZun, Mmabh, 2 M re, Mmabh, ReZun, re bis zum nächsten Mm, LiZun, Mmabh, 2 M re, Mmabh, ReZun, re bis zur letzten M, 1 M verdopp = 64 (66: 66: 70: 70) M.

R 7: 1 M verdopp, re bis zum nächsten Mm, LiZun, Mmabh, 2 M re, Mmabh, ReZun, re bis zum nächsten Mm, LiZun, Mmabh, 2 M re, Mmabh, Rezun, re bis zum nächsten Mm, LiZun, Mmabh, 2 M re, Mmabh, ReZun, re bis zum nächsten Mm, LiZun, Mmabh, 2 M re, Mmabh, ReZun, re bis zur letzten M, 1 M verdopp = 74 (76: 76: 80: 80) M.

Arb wenden, 22 (24: 24: 26: 26) M anschl (für die vord Mitte), einen Mm auf die re Ndl (für Anf und Ende der Rde) = 96 (100: 100: 106: 106) M.

In Runden str wie folgt:

Rde 1: Re.

Rde 2: Re bis zum Mm, *LiZun, Mmabh, 2 M re, Mmabh, ReZun**, re bis zum nächsten Mm, ab * 2 x wdhl, danach von * bis ** noch 1 x wdhl, re bis zum Ende der Rde = 8 Zun = 104 (108: 108: 114: 114) M.

Rde 3: Re.
Die 2 letzten Runden 2 (5: 10: 12: 16) x wdhl = 120 (148: 188: 210: 242) M.

Größe 1, 2, 3, und 4 speziell
Nächste Rde: Re bis zum Mm, *LiZun, Mmabh, 2 M re, Mmabh, ReZun**, re bis zum nächsten Mm, ab * 2 x wdhl, danach von * bis ** noch 1 x wdhl, re bis zum Ende der Rde = 8 Zun = 128 (156: 196: 218: -) M.
Nächste Rde: Re.
Nächste Rde: *Re bis zum Mm, Mmabh, 2 M re, Mmabh, ReZun, re bis zum nächsten Mm, LiZun, Mmabh, 2 M re, Mmabh, ab *noch 1 x wdhl, re bis zum Ende = 4 Zun = 132 (160: 200: 222: -) M.
Nächste Rde: Re.
Die letzten 4 Runden 4 (4: 2: 1: -) x wdhl = 180 (208: 224: 234: -) M.

Größe 1, 4 und 5 speziell
Nächste Rde: Re bis zum Mm, *LiZun, Mmabh, 2 M re, Mmabh, ReZun**, re bis zum nächsten Mm, ab * 2 x wdhl, danach von * bis ** noch 1 x wdhl, re bis zum Ende der Rde = 8 Zun = 188 (242: 250) M.
3 Runden re str.
Die letzten 4 Runden – (-: 1) x wdhl = 188 (242: 258) M.

Alle Größen
Armausschnitte
Nächste Rde: Re bis zum 1. Mm, den Mm entfernen, 1 M re, die nächsten 38 (42: 44: 47: 49) M für den li Ärmel auf einer Hilfsndl stilllegen, dabei die 2 Mm entfernen, 4 M anschl (für den Armausschnitt), dabei einen Mm nach der 2. Anschlagmasche auf die re Ndl (für Anf und Ende der Rde), die nächsten 56 (62: 68: 74: 80) M für das Rückenteil re str, dabei 2 Mm entfernen, die nächsten 38 (42: 44: 47: 49) M für den re Ärmel auf einer 2. Hilfsndl stilllegen, dabei 2 Mm entfernen, 4 M anschl, die nächsten 56 (62: 68: 74: 80) M für das Vorderteil re str, den Mm für die Raglannaht und den Mm für Anf und Ende der Rde entfernen = 120 (132: 144: 156: 168) M für Rücken- und Vorderteil.
In Runden weiter re str bis 34,5 (35,5: 35,5: 36,5: 36,5) cm ab den Armausschnitten erreicht sind.
Wechseln zur langen Rundstrickndl Nr. 5.
Nächste Rde: *1 M re, 1 M li, ab * wdhl bis zum Ende der Rde.
Die letzte Rde 3 x wdhl.
Nächste Rde: Re.
Die letzte Rde 3 x wdhl.
Alle M locker re abk.

ÄRMEL
Die 38 (42: 44: 47: 49) M eines Ärmels auf einem Nadelspiel Nr. 7 gleichmäßig verteilen, und mit neuem Fd re str.
Aus den 4 angeschl M 4 M aufn und re str, dabei nach der 2. M einen Mm auf die re Ndl hängen (für Anf und Ende der Rde) = 42 (46: 48: 51: 53) M.
Größe 2, 3, 4 und 5 speziell
14 (10: 10: 8) Runden str.
Nächste Rde: 1 M re, 2 M re zus-str, re bis zu den letzten 3 M, 2 M re verschr zus-str, 1 M re = 44 (46: 49: 51) M.
Die letzte Rde noch 1 (2: 2: 3) x in jeder folg 14. (12.: 12.: 9.) Rde wdhl = 42 (42: 45: 45) M.
Alle Größen
Weiter re str bis eine Ärmellänge von 32 (32: 33: 33: 33) cm ist, danach das Wellenmuster str wie folgt:
Rde 1-7: Re.

Rde 8: *3 (3: 3: 4: 4) x (die nächste M auf der li Ndl mit der M auf der Rückseite der Arb 7 Runden tiefer re zus-str, 11 M re), ab * wdhl bis zum Ende der Rde.
Rde 9-11: Re.
Rde 12: *3 (3: 3: 4: 4) x 7 M re, (die nächste M auf der li Ndl mit der M auf der Rückseite der Arb 7 Runden tiefer re zus-str), 4 M re, ab * wdhl bis zum Ende der Rde.
Rde 13-17: Re.
Rde 8-17 noch 1 x wdhl, danach Rde 8-12 noch 1 x str.
Nächste Rde: - (-: -: 1: 1) M re, *5 (5: 5: 4: 4) M re, 2 M re zus-str, ab * 5 (5: 5: 6: 6) x wdhl, - (-: -: 2: 2) M re = 36 (36: 36: 38: 38) M re.
Wechseln zum Nadelspiel Nr. 5.
Nächste Rde: *1 M re, 1 M li, ab * wdhl bis zum Ende.
Die letzte Rde 3 x wdhl.
Nächste Rde: Re.
Die letzte Rde 3 x wdhl.
Alle M locker re abk.

FERTIGSTELLUNG
Alle Teile dämpfen, siehe Informationsseite.
Kragen
Von re mit der Rundstrickndl Nr. 6 aus der ganzen Halsausschnittkante 60 (60: 60: 75: 75) M aufn und re str, einen Mm auf die re Ndl.
Im Wellenmuster str wie folgt:
Rde 1-7: Re.
Rde 8: *3 (3: 3: 4: 4) x (die nächste M auf der li Ndl mit der M auf der Rückseite der Arb 7 Runden tiefer re zus-str), 11 M re, ab * wdhl bis zum Ende der Rde.
Rde 9-11: Re.
Rde 12: *3 (3: 3: 4: 4) x 7 M re, (die nächste M auf der li Ndl mit der M auf der Rückseite der Arb 7 Runden tiefer re zus-str), 4 M re, ab * wdhl bis zum Ende der Rde.
Rde 13-17: Re.
Rde 8-17 noch 1 x wdhl, danach Rde 8-12 noch 1 x str.
Nächste Rde: Re str bis zum Ende der Rde, dabei in der Mitte – (-: -: 1: 1) M abn = 70 (70: 70: 74: 74) M.
Wechseln zum Nadelspiel Nr. 5.
Nächste Rde: *1 M re, 1 M li, ab * wdhl bis zum Ende.
Die letzte Rde 3 x wdhl.
Nächste Rde: Re.
Die letzte Rde 3 x wdhl.

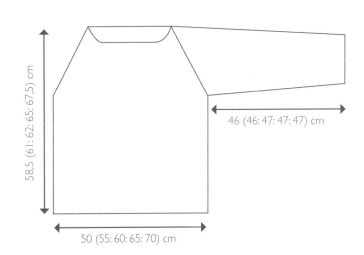

58,5 (61: 62: 65: 67,5) cm
46 (46: 47: 47: 47) cm
50 (55: 60: 65: 70) cm

COCOON ••

Tiam

GRÖSSEN

Passend für Oberweite

81-86	91-97	102-107	112-117	122-127	cm

Gestrickte Oberweite

92	114	137	159	181	cm

GARN

Rowan Big Wool (fotografiert in Glum 056)

11	12	13	14	15	× 100g

NADELN

1 Rundstrickndl Nr. 10, 100-120 cm lang.
1 Nadelspiel Nr. 10

EXTRAS

Fremdgarn für den offenen Anschlag
Maschenmarkierer (Mm)

MASCHENPROBE

9 M und 14 R = 10 × 10 cm, im Perlmuster gestr mit Ndl Nr. 10.
12 M und 15 R = 10 × 10 cm, im 1×1 Rippenmuster gestr mit Ndl Nr. 10.

HINWEIS

Der Body wird wegen der hohen Maschenzahl auf einer Rundstrickndl in Hin- und Rückr gestr.
Die Umrandung, der Bündchenrand und die Taschen werden rund gestr.

BODY

83 (103: 123: 143: 163) M mit Ndl Nr. 10 anschl.
R 1 (Hinr): 1 M re, *1 M li, 1 M re, ab * wdhl bis zum Ende.
Diese R bildet das Perlmuster und wird wdhl bis 10 cm erreicht sind, enden mit einer Rückr.
Taschenöffnung
Nächste R (Hinr): 6 (8: 12: 15: 19) M im Muster, die nächsten 11 M mit dem Fremdgarn str, diese M wieder auf die li Ndl heben und mit dem Arbeitsfaden re str, im Muster str bis zu den letzten 17 (19: 23: 26: 30) M, die nächsten 11 M mit dem Fremdgarn str, diese 11 M wieder auf die li Ndl heben, die M mit dem Arbeitsfaden re str, im Muster str bis zum Ende.
Nächste R (Rückr): Im Perlmuster str bis zum Ende.
Das Muster korrekt einhalten, nach einer Länge von 25 (27,5: 30: 32,5: 35) cm enden mit einer Rückr.

Bündchen

Am Anf der nächsten 2 R je 3 (4: 5: 5: 6) M abk = 77 (95: 113: 133: 151) M.
Gerade str bis eine Gesamtlänge erreicht ist von 35 (37,5: 40: 42,5: 45) cm, enden mit einer Rückr.
Am Anf der nächsten 2 R je 3 (4: 5: 5: 6) M anschl und im Perlmuster str = 83 (103: 123: 143: 163) M.
Nach einer Gesamtlänge von 60 (65: 70: 75: 80) cm enden mit einer Rückr.
Alle M im Muster abk.

FERTIGSTELLUNG

Das Teil dämpfen, siehe Informationsseite.
Den Body in der Länge falten, sodass die Anschlagkante und die Abkettkante aufeinanderliegen, diese Ränder bleiben für die Umrandung offen. Die seitl Ränder (Reihenenden) bis zu den Öffnungen für die Bündchen zusammennähen.
Untere Umrandung
Von re mit der Rundstrickndl Nr. 10 am re seitl Rand beg und aus der Abkettkante bis zum li seitl Rand 110 (137: 164: 190: 217) M aufn und re str, danach aus der Anschlagkante 110 (137: 164: 190: 217) M aufn und re str.
In Runden str wie folgt, dabei Anf und Ende jeder Rde markieren.
Rde 1: *1 M re, 1 M li, ab * wdhl bis zum Ende.
Weiter im Rippenmuster str bis 7 cm erreicht sind, danach alle M locker abk.

Umrandung der Bündchen

Von re mit dem Nadelspiel Nr. 10 aus der ganzen Armausschnittkante 24 M aufn und re str.
In Runden str wie folgt, dabei Anf und Ende jeder Rde markieren.
7 cm im Rippenmuster str, sowie beim Body angegeben, danach alle M locker abk.

Taschen (beide gleich)

Das Fremdgarn bei den Taschenöffnungen vorsichtig entfernen, die je 11 M aus dem oberen und unteren Rand der Öffnung auf einem Nadelspiel Nr. 10 verteilen, mit neuem Fd re str bis zum Ende der Rde. Anf und Ende jeder Rde markieren = 22 M.
Glatt re str bis 9 cm erreicht sind, danach die Taschen auf die Rückseite der Arbeit legen, mit Hilfe einer 3. Ndl die Hälfte der M re zus-str und abk. Die Taschenbeutel an die Anschlagkante des Rippenbündchens an der Halsausschnittkante nähen.

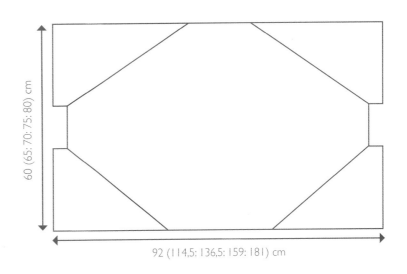

60 (65: 70: 75: 80) cm

92 (114,5: 136,5: 159: 181) cm

SWERVE SCARF ●●●

GRÖSSE
Der Schal ist 25,5 cm breit und 203 cm lang.

GARN
Rowan Big Wool
6 x 100 g
(fotografiert in Normandy 086)

NADELN
1 Paar Nr. 8

MASCHENPROBE
6,5 M und 20 R = nach dem Dämpfen 10 x 10 cm, im Patentmuster gestr mit Ndl Nr. 8

SPEZIELLE ABKÜRZUNGEN
Pre3Mrezus-str/re geneigte Abnahme = 3 M re zus-str (= die nächste re M mit dem Umschlag und die folg li M), die M von der re Ndl wieder auf die li Ndl heben, die beiden folg M (= eine re M mit dem Umschlag) über die 1. M auf der Ndl heben und von der li Ndl fallen lassen, die M von der li Ndl wieder auf die re Ndl heben = 2 Abn.
PreübzAbn/li geneigte Abnahme: 1 M mit dem Umschlag zusammen re abheben, 3 M re zus-str (= die nächste li M mit der folg re M und dem Umschlag), die abgeh M mit dem Umschlag überziehen und von der re Ndl fallen lassen.
Pre2Mrezus-U-Pre2Mrezus/symmetrische Zun: 2 M re zus-str (= die nächste M mit dem Umschlag), die M nicht von der li Ndl fallen lassen, 1 U, 2 M re zus-str (dieselbe M mit dem U noch 1 x str), die restl M von der li Ndl fallen lassen.
Hinweis: In der folg R werden die Zun wie folgt gestr: (1 U, 1 M abh, 1 M re) anstelle von (1 U, 1 M re, 2 M rezus-str).

SCHAL
24 M mit Ndl Nr. 8 anschl.
R 1 (Basis-R): (1 U, 1 M abh, 1 M re) wdhl bis zum Ende.
R 2-8: *1 U, 1 M abh, 2 M re zus-str, ab * wdhl bis zum Ende.
R 9: 9 x (1 U, 1 M abh, 2 M re zus-str), 1 U, 1 M abh, Pre3Mrezus-str, 1 U, 1 M abh, Pre2Mrezus-str-U-Pre2Mrezus.
R 10: 1 U, 1 M abh, 1 M re, *1 U, 1 M abh, 2 M re zus-str, ab *wdhl bis zum Ende.
2 R im Patentmuster str.
R 13: 8 x (1 U, 1 M abh, 2 M re zus-str), 1 U, 1 M abh, Pre3Mrezus, 1 U, 1 M abh, Pre2Mrezus-str-U-Pre2Mrezus, 1 U, 1 M abh, 2 M re zus-str.
R 14: 1 U, 1 M abh, 2 M re zus-str, 1 U, 1 M abh, 1 M re, *1 U, 1 M abh, 2 M re zus-str, ab * wdhl bis zum Ende.
2 R im Patentmuster str.
R 17: 7 x (1 U, 1 M abh, 2 M re zus-str), 1 U, 1 M abh, Pre3Mrezus-str, 1 U, 1 M abh, Pre2Mrezus-str-U-Pre2Mrezus, 2 x (1 U, 1 M abh, 2 M re zus-str).
R 18: 2 x (1 U, 1 M abh, 2 M re zus-str), 1 U, 1 M abh, 1 M re, *1 U, 1 M abh, 2 M re zus-str, ab *wdhl bis zum Ende.
2 R im Patentmuster str.

R 21: 6 x (1 U, 1 M abh, 2 M re zus-str), 1 U, 1 M abh, Pre3Mrezus-str, 1 U, 1 M abh, Pre2Mrezus-str-U-Pre2Mrezus, 3 x (1 U, 1 M abh, 2 M re zus-str).

R 22: 3 x (1 U, 1 M abh, 2 M re zus-str), 1 U, 1 M abh, 1 M re, *1 U, 1 M abh, 2 M re zus-str, ab * wdhl bis zum Ende. 2 R im Patentmuster str.

R 25: 5 x (1 U, 1 M abh, 2 M re zus-str), 1 U, 1 M abh, Pre3Mrezus-str, 1 U, 1 M abh, Pre2Mrezus-str-U-Pre2Mrezus, 4 x (1 U, 1 M abh, 2 M re zus-str).

R 26: 4 x (1 U, 1 M abh, 2 M re zus-str), 1 U, 1 M abh, 1 M re, *1 U, 1 M abh, 2 M re zus-str, ab * wdhl bis zum Ende. 2 R im Patentmuster str.

R 29: 4 x (1 U, 1 M abh, 2 M re zus-str), 1 U, 1 M abh, Pre3Mrezus-str, 1 U, 1 M abh, Pre2Mrezus-str-U-Pre2Mrezus, 5 x (1 U, 1 M abh, 2 M re zus-str).

R 30: 5 x (1 U, 1 M abh, 2 M re zus-str), 1 U, 1 M abh, 1 M re, *1 U, 1 M abh, 2 M re zus-str, ab wdhl bis zum Ende. 2 R im Patentmuster str.

R 33: 3 x (1 U, 1 M abh, 2 M re zus-str), 1 U, 1 M abh, Pre3Mrezus-str, 1 U, 1 M abh, Pre2Mrezus-str-U-Pre2Mrezus, 6 x (1 U, 1 M abh, 2 M re zus-str).

R 34: 6 x (1 U, 1 M abh, 2 M re zus-str), 1 U, 1 M abh, 1 M re, *1 U, 1 M abh, 2 M re zus-str, ab * wdhl bis zum Ende. 2 R im Patentmuster str.

R 37: 2 x (1 U, 1 M abh, 2 M re zus-str), 1 U, 1 M abh, Pre3Mrezus-str, 1 U, 1 M abh, Pre2Mrezus-str-U-Pre2Mrezus, 7 x (1 U, 1 M abh, 2 M re zus-str).

R 38: 7 x (1 U, 1 M abh, 2 M re zus-str), 1 U, 1 M abh, 1 M re, *1 U, 1 M abh, 2 M re zus-str, ab * wdhl bis zum Ende. 2 R im Patentmuster str.

R 41: 1 U, 1 M abh, 2 M re zus-str, 1 U, 1 M abh, Pre3Mrezus-str, 1 U, 1 M abh, Pre2Mrezus-str-U-Pre2Mrezus, 8 x (1 U, 1 M abh, 2 M re zus-str).

R 42: 8 x (1 U, 1 M abh, 2 M re zus-str), 1 U, 1 M abh, 1 M re, *1 U, 1 M abh, 2 M re zus-str, ab * wdhl bis zum Ende. 2 R im Patentmuster str.

R 45: 1 U, 1 M abh, Pre3Mrezus-str, 1 U, 1 M abh, Pre2Mrezus-str-U-Pre2Mrezus, 9 x (1 U, 1 M abh, 2 M re zus-str).

R 46: 9 x (1 U, 1 M abh, 2 M re zus-str), 1 U, 1 M abh, 1 M re, *1 U, 1 M abh, 2 M re zus-str, ab * wdhl bis zum Ende. 2 R im Patentmuster str.

R 49: 1 U, 1 M abh, Pre2Mrezus-str-U-Pre2Mrezus, 1 U, PreübzAbn, 9 x (1 U, 1 M abh, 2 M re zus-str).

R 50: 10 x (1 U, 1 M abh, 2 M re zus-str), 1 U, 1 M abh, 1 M re, (1 U, 1 M abh, 2 M re zus-str) wdhl bis zum Ende. 2 R im Patentmuster str.

R 53: 1 U, 1 M abh, 2 M re zus, 1 U, 1 M abh, Pre2Mrezus-str-U-Pre2Mrezus, 1 U, 1 M abh, PreübzAbn, 8 x (1 U, 1 M abh, 2 M re zus-str).

R 54: 8 x (1 U, 1 M abh, 2 M re zus-str), 1 U, 1 M abh, 1 M re, *1 U, 1 M abh, 2 M re zus-str, ab * wdhl bis zum Ende. 2 R im Patentmuster str.

R 57: 2 x (1 U, 1 M abh, 2 M re zus), 1 U, 1 M abh, Pre2Mrezus-str-U-Pre2Mrezus, 1 U, 1 M abh, PreübzAbn, 7 x (1 U, 1 M abh, 2 M re zus-str).

R 58: 7 x (1 U, 1 M abh, 2 M re zus-str), 1 U, 1 M abh, 1 M re, *1 U, 1 M abh, 2 M re zus-str, ab * wdhl bis zum Ende. 2 R im Patentmuster str.

R 61: 3 x (1 U, 1 M abh, 2 M re zus), 1 U, 1 M abh, Pre2Mrezus-str-U-Pre2Mrezus, 1 U, 1 M abh, PreübzAbn, 6 x (1 U, 1 M abh, 2 M re zus-str).

R 62: 6 x (1 U, 1 M abh, 2 M re zus-str), 1 U, 1 M abh, 1 M re, *1 U, 1 M abh, 2 M re zus-str, ab * wdhl bis zum Ende. 2 R im Patentmuster str.

R 65: 4 x (1 U, 1 M abh, 2 M re zus), 1 U, 1 M abh, Pre2Mrezus-str-U-Pre2Mrezus, 1 U, 1 M abh, PreübzAbn, 5 x (1 U, 1 M abh, 2 M re zus-str).

R 66: 5 x (1 U, 1 M abh, 2 M re zus-str), 1 U, 1 M abh, 1 M re, *1 U, 1 M abh, 2 M re zus-str, ab * wdhl bis zum Ende. 2 R im Patentmuster str.

R 69: 5 x (1 U, 1 M abh, 2 M re zus), 1 U, 1 M abh, Pre2Mrezus-str-U-Pre2Mrezus, 1 U, 1 M abh, PreübzAbn, 4 x (1 U, 1 M abh, 2 M re zus-str).

R 70: 4 x (1 U, 1 M abh, 2 M re zus-str), 1 U, 1 M abh, 1 M re, *1 U, 1 M abh, 2 M re zus-str, ab * wdhl bis zum Ende. 2 R im Patentmuster str.

R 73: 6 x (1 U, 1 M abh, 2 M re zus), 1 U, 1 M abh, Pre2Mrezus-str-U-Pre2Mrezus, 1 U, 1 M abh, PreübzAbn, 3 x (1 U, 1 M abh, 2 M re zus-str).

R 74: 3 x (1 U, 1 M abh, 2 M re zus-str), 1 U, 1 M abh, 1 M re, *1 U, 1 M abh, 2 M re zus-str, ab * wdhl bis zum Ende. 2 R im Patentmuster str.

R 77: 7 x (1 U, 1 M abh, 2 M re zus), 1 U, 1 M abh, Pre2Mrezus-str-U-Pre2Mrezus, 1 U, 1 M abh, PreübzAbn, 2 x (1 U, 1 M abh, 2 M re zus-str).

R 78: 2 x (1 U, 1 M abh, 2 M re zus-str), 1 U, 1 M abh, 1 M re, *1 U, 1 M abh, 2 M re zus-str, ab * wdhl bis zum Ende. 2 R im Patentmuster str.

R 81: 8 x (1 U, 1 M abh, 2 M re zus), 1 U, 1 M abh, Pre2Mrezus-str-U-Pre2Mrezus, 1 U, 1 M abh, PreübzAbn, 1 U, 1 M abh, 2 M re zus-str.

R 82: 1 U, 1 M abh, 2 M re zus-str, 1 U, 1 M abh, 1 M re, *1 U, 1 M abh, 2 M re zus-str, ab * wdhl bis zum Ende. 2 R im Patentmuster str.

R 85: 9 x (1 U, 1 M abh, 2 M re zus), 1 U, 1 M abh, Pre2Mrezus-str-U-Pre2Mrezus, 1 U, 1 M abh, PreübzAbn.

R 86: 1 U, 1 M abh, 1 M re, *1 U, 1 M abh, 2 M re zus-str, ab * wdhl bis zum Ende. 6 R im Patentmuster str.

R 9-86 werden 4 x wdhl (= 5 Rapporte insgesamt). Weitere 2 R im Patentmuster str.

Abkettreihe: 1 M li, (2 M re zus-str, die li M überziehen, 1 M li, die M überziehen) wdhl bis zu den letzten 2 M, 2 M re zus-str, die M überziehen, den Fd abschneiden.

SWERVE BEANIE •

GRÖSSE
Passend für eine durchschnittliche Kopfgröße

GARN
Rowan Big Wool
2 x 100 g
(fotografiert in Normandy 086)

NADELN
1 Nadelspiel Nr. 7

MASCHENPROBE
10.5 M und 24 R = 10 x 10 cm, im Patentmuster gestr mit Ndl Nr. 8.

Zu- und Abnahmen im Patentmuster
Pre3Mrezus-str/re geneigte Abnahme = 3 M re zus-str (= die nächste re M mit dem Umschlag und die folg li M), die M von der re Ndl wieder auf die li Ndl heben, die beiden folg M (= eine re M mit dem Umschlag) über die 1. M auf der Ndl heben und von der li Ndl fallen lassen, die M von der li Ndl wieder auf die re Ndl heben = 2 Abn.
Pre2Mrezus-U-Pre2zus/symmetrische Zun: 2 M re zus-str (= die nächste M mit dem Umschlag), die M nicht von der li Ndl fallen lassen, 1 U, 2 M re zus-str (dieselbe M mit dem U noch 1 x str), die restl M von der li Ndl fallen lassen. **Hinweis:** In der folg R werden die Zun wie folgt gestr: 1 U, 1 M abh, 1 M re anstelle von 1 U, 1 M re, 2 M rezus-str,

50 M mit Ndl Nr. 7 anschl, in Runden str wie folgt:
Rde 1 (re Basis-Rde 1): (1 M re, 1 U, 1 M abh, wdhl bis zum Ende (Der Umschlag wird musterbedingt gestr und wird nicht als Zun gestr).
Rde 2 (li Basis-Rde 2): (1 U, 1 M abh, 2 M li zus-str) wdhl bis zum Ende.

Rde 3: (2 M re zus-str, 1 U, 1 M abh) wdhl bis zum Ende. Rde 2 und 3 noch 1 x wdhl, danach Rde 2 noch 1 x str.
Rde 7: 5 x [2 x (2 M re zus-str, 1 U, 1 M abh), Pre3Mrezus-str, 1 U, 1 M abh, Pre2Mrezus-str-U-Pre2Mrezus-str, 1 U, 1 M abh].
Rde 8: 5 x [3 x (1 U, 1 M abh, 2 M li zus-str), 1 U, 1 M abh, 1 M li, 1 x (1 U, 1 M abh, 2 M li zus-str)].
Rde 9: Wie Rde 3.
Rde 10: Wie Rde 2.
Rde 11: 5 x [1 x (2 M re zus-str, 1 U, 1 M abh), Pre3Mrezus-str, 1 U, 1 M re, Pre2Mrezus-str-U-Pre2Mrezus-str, 1 U, 1 M abh, 1 x (2 M re zus-str, 1 U, 1 M abh].
Rde 12: 5 x [2 x (1 U, 1 M abh, 2 M li zus-str), 1 U, 1 M abh, 1 M li, 2 x (1 U, 1 M abh, 2 M li zus-str].
Rde 13: Wie Rde 3.
Rde 14: Wie Rde 2.
Rde 15: 5 x [Pre3Mrezus-str, 1 U, 1 M abh, Pre2Mrezus-str-U-Pre2Mrezus-str, 1 U, 1 M abh, 2 x (2 M re zus-str, 1 U, 1 M abh)].
Rde 16: 5 x [1 x (1 U, 1 M abh, 2 M li zus-str), 1 U, 1 M abh, 1 M li, 3 x (1 U, 1 M abh, 3 M li zus-str)].
Weiter im Patentmuster = Rde 3 und 2 im Wechsel, bis 18 cm erreicht sind, enden mit Rde 2 des Musters.
Nächste Rde: 5 x [3 x (2 M re zus-str, 1 U, 1 M abh), Pre3Mrezus, 1 U, 1 M abh] = 40 M (ohne Umschläge).
Nächste Rde: Wie Rde 2.
Nächste Rde: Wie Rde 3.
Nächste Rde: Wie Rde 2.
Nächste Rde: 5 x [2 x (2 M re zus-str, 1 U, 1 M abh), Pre3Mrezus, 1 U, 1 M abh] = 30 M (ohne Umschläge).
Nächste Rde: Wie Rde 2.
Nächste Rde: Wie Rde 3.
Nächste Rde: Wie Rde 2.
Nächste Rde: 5 x [1 x (2 M re zus-str, 1 U, 1 M abh), Pre3Mrezus, 1 U, 1 M abh] = 20 M (ohne Umschläge).
Nächste Rde: Wie Rde 2.
Nächste Rde: Wie Rde 3.
Nächste Rde: Wie Rde 2.
Nächste Rde: 5 x (2 M re zus-str, 1 U, 1 M abh), = 10 M (ohne Umschläge).
Nächste Rde: (1 M re, 2 M li zus-str) wdhl bis zum Ende = 7 M. Den Fd abschneiden und durch die restl M ziehen, die M fest zusammenziehen, den Fd gut vernähen.

ALLGEMEINE HINWEISE

Maschenprobe

Die Einhaltung der richtigen Maschenprobe ist wahrscheinlich der wichtigste Faktor, der den Unterschied zwischen einem gelungenen Meisterwerk und einem verpatzten Kleidungsstück ausmacht. Form und Größe, aber auch Fall und Sitz des Gestrickten hängen von ihr ab, daher können bereits kleinste Abweichungen die Gesamtwirkung zerstören.

Am Anfang jeder Anleitung steht die tatsächliche Maschenprobe des Designers und diese müssen Sie einhalten. Es kann sogar sein, daß für ein Strickstück mehrere Maschenproben genannt werden, wenn Teile der Arbeit in Intarsientechnik, andere Teile glatt rechts und wieder andere in Jacquard-Technik gestrickt sind. Wir raten Ihnen dringend eine Strickprobe im jeweiligen Muster zu stricken, die 5-10 Maschen breiter und 5-10 Reihen länger ist als in der Maschenprobe angegeben. Legen Sie diese Strickprobe flach auf den Tisch und messen Sie sie in ihrer Mitte ab. Wenn Sie zu viele Maschen auf 10 cm zählen, stricken Sie eine neue Maschenprobe, bei der Sie dickere Nadeln verwenden. Zählen Sie weniger Maschen auf 10 cm, versuchen Sie es noch einmal mit dünneren Nadeln. Die Angaben über Nadelstärken in den Anleitungen sind nur sehr ungenaue Orientierungshilfen, da jeder eine andere Fadenspannung hat und die Maschen dadurch von Person zu Person unterschiedlich groß werden.

Größen

Bei vielen Anleitungen sind mehrere Größen angegeben. Steht nur eine Zahl da, gilt sie für alle Größen, sind mehrere Zahlen hintereinander angegeben, gilt die erste für die kleinste Größe und die restlichen in Klammern jeweils für die dann folgenden größeren Größen. Die kleine Schnittzeichnung am Ende jeder Anleitung zeigt die fertig gestrickten Maße, außerdem finden Sie eine genaue Größentabelle auf der vorherigen Seite.

Zählmuster

Einige der Modelle in diesem Heft werden nach einem Zählmuster gearbeitet. Darin steht jedes Kästchen für eine Masche und jede Kästchenreihe für eine Strickreihe. Beim Stricken nach den Zählmustern werden die Hinreihen von rechts nach links gelesen und gestrickt, die Rückreihen von links nach rechts, falls nicht anders angegeben. Jede verwendete Farbe ist durch ein eigenes Symbol oder einen eigenen Buchstaben gekennzeichnet. Zur Erleichterung der Arbeit können Sie das Diagramm vergrößert fotokopieren und die benötigte Größe, auch im Text, farbig markieren.

Lochmuster

Beim Lochmuster müssen immer ebenso viele Umschläge gestrickt werden, wie Maschen zusammen gestrickt werden. Sollten, bedingt durch die seitlichen Ab- oder Zunahmen für die Formgebung an den Rändern nicht mehr genügend Maschen für eine vollständige Musterfolge vorhanden sein, werden die restlichen Maschen solange glatt rechts gestrickt, bis wieder genug Maschen für eine Musterfolge vorhanden sind. Eine Hilfe ist es, links und rechts des vollständigen Musters je einen Markierungsring einzuhängen.

Stricken mit Farben

Für das Arbeiten mit Fraben gibt es zwei Haupttechniken: Intarsientechnik und Norweger- oder Fair-Isle Technik. Mit der ersten Technik erhalten Sie einen einlagigen Stoff und sie wird meist nur dann verwendet, wenn Farbe an einer bestimmten Stelle gestrickt wird. Die Norweger- oder Fair-Isle Technik hingegen produziert einen dickeren Stoff, da mehr als eine Farbe durchgehend über die ganze Reihe gestrickt wird.

Intarsientechnik

Am einfachsten geht es, wenn man für jedes Motiv oder für jedes Farbfeld kürzere Fäden der benötigten Farben abschneidet (je nach Größe des Motivs 50 cm bis 3 m lange Fäden, die auf der Rückseite hängen bleiben, wenn sie nicht benötigt werden), – so verhindert man, dass sich die Knäuel verknoten. Bei jedem Farbwechsel innerhalb der Reihe werden die Fäden miteinander verkreuzt, damit keine Löcher entstehen. Die Enden der Fäden können am Schluss entlang der Farbwechsel vernäht oder beim Stricken "eingewebt" werden. Das Einweben erfolgt nach dem gleichen Prinzip wie das Einweben bei der Norwegertechnik, und erspart das zeitraubende Vernähen der Fäden. Bei der Intarsientechnik ist zu beachten, dass die Maschenprobe von einer glatt rechts gestrickten einfarbigen Maschenprobe abweichen kann.

Norweger- oder Fair-Isle Technik

Wenn zwei oder drei Farben im Laufe einer Reihe ständig wiederholt werden, nehmen Sie den oder die gerade nicht benötigten Fäden locker gespannt auf der Rückseite der Arbeit mit. Wenn Sie mit mehr als zwei Farben arbeiten, behandeln Sie die mitgeführten Fäden wie einen einzigen Faden und dehnen Sie die Maschen immer wieder auf ihre richtige Weite aus, damit die Fäden locker genug, aber nicht zu locker hängen. Spannen Sie die mitgeführten Fäden nie über mehr als drei Maschen, sondern geben Sie den Spannfäden Halt, indem Sie sie bei jeder 2. oder 3. Masche einweben, d. h. umfassen Sie sie abwechselnd unter und über dem Arbeitsfaden. Dadurch werden sie auf der Rückseite der Arbeit festgehalten.

Fertigstellung

Nachdem so viele Stunden an einem Strickstück gestrickt wurde, ist es schade, dass so viele Modelle durch die falsche Behandlung beim Bügeln verdorben werden. Hier einige Tipps für eine wirklich perfekte Konfektionierung.

Dämpfen

Nach Abschluss der Arbeit werden alle Fäden vernäht und alle Strickteile einzeln auf einer weichen Unterlage mit rostfreien Stecknadeln aufgesteckt (oberhalb der eventuellen Rippenmusterbereiche) und mit einem feuchten Tuch bedeckt. Wenn das Tuch trocken ist, ist die Arbeit auf sanfte Art in Form gebracht, ohne dabei ihr Volumen und ihre lebendige Struktur zu verlieren, wie das beim vielfach empfohlenen Bügeln unter einem feuchten Tuch leicht der Fall ist. Beachten Sie auch immer die Hinweise auf der Banderole.

Zusammennähen

Beim Zusammennähen der Teile achten Sie auf genaue Übereinstimmung der Farben. Sie können die Teile sehr sorgfältig von links mit Steppstichen (besonders Armkugel und schräge Schulternähte) verbinden oder von rechts im Matratzenstich zusammennähen. Dieser empfiehlt sich besonders bei geraden Nähten, Bündchen und feinteiligen Farbmustern. Für die Befestigung von Blenden und Taschenbeuteln auf der Innenseite eines Strickstücks ist vielfach der Maschenstich die unauffälligste Lösung.

Für die Ärmel gibt es verschiedene Methoden des Einsetzens.

Beim Ärmel ohne Armkugel wird der Ärmel mit der Mitte der oberen Ärmelkante auf die Schulternaht geheftet und in der angegebenen Armausschnitthöhe am Vorder- und Rückenteil eingenäht, danach werden die Ärmel- und Seitennähte geschlossen.

Beim Ärmel mit L-Ausschnitt wird die Mitte der oberen Ärmelkante auf die Schulternaht geheftet und der Ärmel bis zum Beginn der Abnahmen für die Armausschnitte in die Armausschnittkante eingenäht. Anschließend werden die letzten geraden Reihen des Ärmels mit den Abnahmen der Armausschnittkante verbunden.

Beim Ärmel mit Armkugel werden zuerst die Seitennähte von Vorder- und Rückenteil geschlossen. Die Mitte der Armkugel wird auf die Schulternaht geheftet, danach wird der Ärmel mit eingehaltener Weite in den Armausschnitt genäht.

Die Seiten- und Unterarmnähte schließen.
Die Taschenblenden und Taschenbeutel festnähen.
Die Knöpfe in Höhe der Knopflöcher festnähen.
Gerippte Bündchen oder Halsblenden sowie kraus rechts gestrickte Abschnitte dürfen nicht gedämpft werden.

Abkürzungen

Abk	abketten
abn	abnehmen
Anf	Anfang
anschl	anschlagen
arb	arbeiten
bds	beidseitig
Fbe	Farbe
Hinr	Hinreihe
li	links
M	Masche
mark	markieren
Ndl	Nadel
Nr.	Nummer
R	Reihe
Rde	Runde
re	rechts
Rückr	Rückreihe
seitl	seitlich
str	stricken
U	Umschlag
verschr	verschränkt
vord	vordere
wdhl	wiederholen
ZN	Zopfnadel
zun	zunehmen
zus-str	zusammenstricken

Experience Bewertungen

• = Für Anfänger
Für Anfänger mit Grundkenntnissen geeignet, gerade Passform mit unkomplizierter Maschentechnik.

• • = Einfache Technik
Einfache, unkomplizierte Stricktechnik mit einer Einweisung in verschiedene Schnitttechniken bei der Fertigung von Strickstücken.

• • • = Schwierige Techniken
Für erfahrenere Stricker, die gerne anspruchsvollere Techniken mit mehrfarbigen Mustern verwenden.

• • • • = Für Fortgeschrittene
Für Stricker, die gerne nach Schnitten mit herausfordernden Techniken und Mustern arbeiten.

Alle im Magazin angegebenen Knöpfe und Bänder sind erhältlich bei

Groves & Banks
Eastern Bypass
Thame
Oxfordshire
OX9 3FU
www.grovesltd.co.uk
groves@stockistenquiries.co.uk

Bedecked Haberdashery
The Coach House
Barningham Park
RICHMOND
DL11 7DW
Tel: +44 (0)1833 621 451
eMail:Judith.lewis@bedecked.co.uk
www.bedecked.co.uk

Hinweise zur Pflege

Sie haben sicher bemerkt, dass sich in der letzten Saison die Symbole zur Pflege auf den Banderolen und Farbkarten geändert haben. Wir haben die Symbole aktualisiert, sie sollen Ihnen eine Hilfe sein zur weiteren Pflege für Ihre gestrickten oder gehäkelten Modelle. Unten sehen Sie die Symbole mit einer kurzen Erklärung.

Symbole für die Waschmaschine

Symbole für die Handwäsche

Symbole für chemisches Reinigen

Symbole zum Bügeln

Symbol für das Verwenden von Bleichmitteln

Symbole für den Trockner

GRÖSSENTABELLE

Wenn Sie ein Rowan Modell stricken und tragen wollen, wünschen wir, dass es gut aussieht und Sie sich darin wohl fühlen. Das alles beginnt mit der Wahl der richtigen Größe. Wir helfen Ihnen, eine erfahrene Stricker/in zu werden, weswegen wir uns die im Heft angegebenen Größen der Damen- und Herrenmodelle angesehen haben. Im Resultat sehen Sie unten eine Einführung in unsere neue Maßtabelle mit speziellen Hinweisen.

Unsere Größen beruhen auf den Standardgrößen der Fertigkonfektionen. Wenn Sie Konfektionsgröße 38 tragen, dann ist in der Anleitung die Größe M richtig.

Die Herrengrößen sind jetzt angegeben von XS bis 2 XL, das entspricht einem Brustumfang von 97 – 127 cm.

Außerdem haben wir jetzt noch eine UNISEX Größe angegeben. Es sind die gleichen Größen wie bei den Herren Standardgrößen angegeben, hinzu kommt noch XXS.

Die in den untenstehenden Listen angegebenen Größen sind immer Körpergrößen, und nicht die gestrickten Größen, so sollen Ihnen die Maßtabellen dabei behilflich sein, die richtige Größe zu finden.

STANDARD DAMENGRÖSSEN

Zusätzlich zu den Standardgrößen sind die einzelnen Konfektionsgrößen angegeben d.h. Größe M entspricht Größe 38.

UK SIZE	S	M	L	XL	XXL	
EUR Größe	36-38	38-40	40-42	42-44	44-46	
Oberweite	81 – 86	91 - 97	102 – 107	112 – 117	122 – 127	cm
Taillenweite	61 – 66	71 – 76	81 – 86	91 – 97	102 – 107	cm
Hüftwweite	86 – 91	97 – 102	107 – 112	117 – 122	127 – 132	cm

STANDARDGRÖSSEN FÜR MÄNNER UND UNISEX GRÖSSENTABELLE

Herrengrößen von XS bis 2 XL. Unisex Größen: XXS bis XL

UK SIZE	XXS	XS	S	M	L	XL	XXL	2XL	
EUR Größe	46	48	50	52	54	56	58	60	
Oberweite	91	97	102	107	112	117	122	127	cm
Taillenweite	71	76	81	86	91	97	102	107	cm

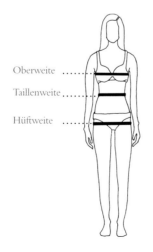

Oberweite ....

Taillenweite ....

Hüftweite ....

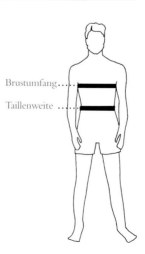

Brustumfang....

Taillenweite ....

GRÖSSEN UND HINWEIS ZU DEN DIAGRAMMEN

Die Anleitungen werden immer für die kleinste Größe geschrieben. Wenn die Zahlen abweichen, stehen die Zahlen für die nächsten Größen in Klammern hinter der kleinsten Größe. Steht nur eine Zahl da, bezieht sie sich auf alle Größen. Zu allen Anleitungen finden Sie unten rechts ein Schnittdiagramm, es zeigt die Maße für das fertige Modell an. Die Zahlen am unteren Rand beziehen sich auf die Breite 2,5 cm unterhalb der Armausschnitte. Um ihre richtige

Größe zu finden, sollten Sie erst in der Maßtabelle Ihre Maße mit den angegebenen Zahlen vergleichen. Generell ist der untere Rand eines Modells genauso breit wie die Oberweite. Allerdings haben manche Designs eine A-Form oder einen abgerundeten Rand, dann kann der Rand breitet sein als die angegebene Oberweite.

RICHTIGES MASSNEHMEN

Für maximalen Tragekomfort und korrekte Passform beachten Sie bitte folgende Tipps.
Messen Sie Ihre Größen eng am Körper über der Unterwäsche, das Maßband dabei nicht zu fest ziehen.

Oberweite: Die Oberweite wird über der breitesten Stelle der Brust gemessen und den Schulterblättern gemessen.

Taille: Die Taille wird direkt über dem Hüftknochen in der natürlich verlaufenden Taille gemessen.

Hüfte: Die Hüfte wird über der breitesten Stelle der Hüfte gemrssen.

Wenn Sie selbst nicht Maß nehmen können, dann nehmen Sie Ihren Lieblingspullover. Unsere Maße entsprechen der handelsüblichen Konfektionen, wenn also Ihr Lieblinspullover die Größe 38 hat, müsste Größe M ungefähr die gleichen Maße haben.
Um sicher zu gehen, dass Ihr Lieblinspullover und die angegebenen

Größen in der Rowan Maßtabelle übereinstimmen, vergleichen Sie die Zahlen mit den individuellen Anleitungen.

Schließlich, wenn Sie die richtige Größe gefunden haben, empfehlen wir Ihnen, eine Maschenprobe für jedes Modell anzufertigen, das Sie stricken möchten.
Sollte die Maschenprobe zu locker sein, wird das Strickstück größer und die angegebene Wollmenge reicht nicht aus, ist sie zu fest, wird das Strickstück zu eng und es bleibt Wolle übrig.

Hinzu kommt, dass, wenn die Maschenprobe nicht korrekt ist, das Strickstück entweder zu fest oder zu locker wird. Es ist wirklich wichtig, vor dem Beginn eines Projektes eine exakte Maschenprobe anzufertigen.

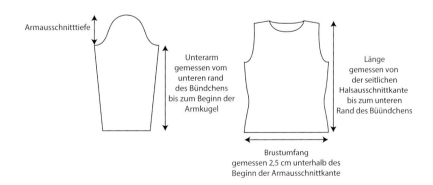

Armausschnitttiefe

Unterarm gemessen vom unteren rand des Bündchens bis zum Beginn der Armkugel

Länge gemessen von der seitlichen Halsausschnittkante bis zum unteren Rand des Büündchens

Brustumfang gemessen 2,5 cm unterhalb des Beginn der Armausschnittkante

DISTRIBUTORS

AUSTRALIA: Morris and Sons
Level 1, 234 Collins Street, Melbourne Vic 3000
Tel: 03 9654 0888 **Web:** morrisandsons.com.au

AUSTRALIA: Morris and Sons
50 York Street, Sydney NSW 2000
Tel: 02 92998588 **Web:** morrisandsons.com.au

AUSTRIA: DMC
5 Avenue de Suisse BP 189, Illzach (France)
Email: info-FR@dmc.com

BELGIUM: DMC
5 Avenue de Suisse BP 189, Illzach (France)
Email: info-FR@dmc.com

CANADA: Sirdar USA Inc.
406 20th Street SE, Hickory, North Carolina, USA 28602
Tel: 828 404 3705 **Email:** sirdarusa@sirdar.co.uk

CHINA: Commercial Agent Mr Victor Li,
Email: victor.li@mezcrafts.com

CHINA: Shanghai Yujun CO.LTD.
Room 701 Wangjiao Plaza, No.175 Yan'an Road, 200002 Shanghai, China
Tel: +86 2163739785 **Email:** jessechang@vip.163.com

DENMARK: Carl J. Permin A/S
Egegaardsvej 28 DK-2610 Rødovre
Tel: (45) 36 36 89 89 **Email:** permin@permin.dk
Web: www.permin.dk

ESTONIA: Mez Crafts Estonia OÜ
Helgi tee 2, Peetri alevik, Tallinn, 75312 Harjumaa
Tel: +372 6 306 759 Email: info.ee@mezcrafts.com
Web: www.mezcrafts.ee

FINLAND: Prym Consumer Finland Oy
Huhtimontie 6, 04200 KERAVA
Tel: +358 9 274871 **Email:** sales.fi@prym.com

FRANCE: DMC
5 Avenue de Suisse BP 189, Illzach (France)
Email: info-FR@dmc.com

GERMANY: DMC
5 Avenue de Suisse BP 189, Illzach (France)
Email: info-DE@dmc.com

HOLLAND: G. Brouwer & Zn B.V.
Oudhuijzerweg 69, 3648 AB Wilnis
Tel: 0031 (0) 297-281 557 **Email:** info@gbrouwer.nl

ICELAND: Carl J. Permin A/S
Egegaardsvej 28, DK-2610 Rødovre
Tel: (45) 36 72 12 00 **Email:** permin@permin.dk
Web: www.permin.dk

ITALY: DMC
Via Magenta 77/5, Rho (Milano)
Email: info-IT@dmc.com

JAPAN: DMC KK
Santo Building 7F, 13, Kanda Konya Cho, Chiyodaku, 101-0035 , Tokyo
Email: ouchi@dmc-kk.com

KOREA: My Knit Studio
3F, 59 Insadong-gil, Jongno-gu, 03145, Seoul
Tel: 82-2-722-0006 **Email:** myknit@myknit.com
Web: www.myknit.com

LATVIA: Latvian Crafts
12-2, Jurģu street, LV-2011
Tel: +371 37 126326825 **Email:** vjelkins@latviancrafts.lv
Web: www.latviancrafts.lv

LEBANON: y.knot
Saifi Village, Mkhalissiya Street 162, Beirut
Tel: (961) 1 992211 **Email:** y.knot@cyberia.net.lb

LUXEMBOURG: DMC
5 Avenue de Suisse BP 189, Illzach (France)
Email: info-FR@dmc.com

NEW ZEALAND: Trendy Trims
7 Angle Street, Onehunga, Auckland, New Zealand
Email: trendy@trendytrims.co.nz **Web:** trendytrims.co.nz

NORWAY: Carl J. Permin A/S
Andersrudveien 1, 1914, Ytre Enebakk
Tel: 23 16 35 30 **Email:** permin@permin.dk
Web: www.permin.dk

PORTUGAL: DMC
P. Ferrocarriles Catalanes, 117 oficina 34, Cornellá de llobregat, 08940
Email: info-PT @dmc.com

RUSSIA: Family Hobby
Zelenograd, Haus 1505, Raum III, 124683
Email: tv@fhobby.ru **Web:** www.family-hobby.ru

SOUTH AFRICA: Arthur Bales LTD
62 4th Avenue, Linden 2195
Tel: (27) 11 888 2401 **Email:** info@arthurbales.co.za
Web: www.arthurbales.co.za

SPAIN: DMC
P. Ferrocarriles Catalanes, 117 oficina 34, Cornellá de llobregat, 08940
Email: info-SP @dmc.com

SWEDEN: Carl J. Permin A/S
Skaraborgsvägen 35C, 3tr, Borås
Tel: 33 12 77 10 **Email:** sverige@permin.dk
Web: www.permin.dk

SWITZERLAND: DMC
5 Avenue de Suisse BP 189, Illzach (France)
Email: info-DE@dmc.com

U.S.A.: Sirdar USA Inc
406 20th Street SE, Hickory, North Carolina, USA 28602
Tel: 828 404 3705 **Email:** sirdarusa@sirdar.co.uk
Web: www.sirdar.com

U.K: Rowan
Flanshaw Lane, Alverthorpe, Wakefield, WF2 9ND, United Kingdom
Tel: 01924 371501 **Email:** mail@knitrowan.com

For more stockists in all countries please logon to **www.knitrowan.com**